To Amy
Birthday [illegible])
friend in South-Africa.

<u>Happy</u> Birthday! 6/10/1988

The Golden Escarpment

The story of the Eastern Transvaal

During fireside chats with Arthur Evans – we were negotiating the acquisition of Mount Sheba at the time – I listened with great pleasure and growing interest to the anecdotes he was able to relate about the area and its past. I learnt that there was a wealth of fascinating information stored away in the memories of the older generation of residents, and it seemed a pity not to capture and commit to paper these first-hand stories before it was too late.

Thus, in an effort to preserve local history – and to encourage an awareness of the ecological importance of the Eastern Transvaal – this book was commissioned and sponsored by Mount Sheba and its holding company, Ovland.

In keeping with this commitment to conservation, half the proceeds of the book will be donated to the Wilderness Leadership School in support of the highly laudable principles it holds and the outstanding work it does.

TINY BARNETSON
CHAIRMAN, MOUNT SHEBA

This book was
financed by Mount Sheba,
an Ovland development

The Golden Escarpment

The story of the Eastern Transvaal

Photography by Pat Evans
Text edited by Peter Joyce

C. Struik, Cape Town

C. Struik (Pty) Ltd
Struik House, Oswald Pirow Street
Foreshore, Cape Town 8001
Reg. No. 80/02842/07

First published 1986

Designed by Joanne Simpson, Cape Town
Original research for text by Marion Giessen
Edited by Peter Joyce
Reproduction and typesetting by Hirt & Carter, Cape Town
Printed and bound by National Book Printers, Cape Town

Photographer's Acknowledgements

The photographer would like to record her grateful thanks
to the following people who helped her during the making of this book:
the *Library* and *Museum Services* of the Transvaal Provincial Administration;
the curator of the Pilgrim's Rest Museum, *Peter Coston,*
and the museum's guide, *Corrie Middel;*
Dr W. G. Winkler of the Sabie Forestry Museum;
Jacqui King of the Lydenburg Museum;
Don Curle of de Kuilen Fisheries;
André Engelbrecht of Bourke's Luck;
Tiny Barnetson (managing director) and *Lola Soucek* (receptionist) of Mount Sheba Hotel;
Arthur and *Ursula Evans* and *Dieter Heinsohn* of Mount Sheba Nature Reserve;
Mike and *Rhoda Owens* of Pilgrim's Rest;
Rickie and *Doreen Pott* of Sabie;
Ken, Yvonne and *Joss Gamble* and *Claude Charles Cogill* of Mali-dyke Gold Mine;
Etta Judson of Lydenburg;
Dr John Rourke of the Kirstenbosch Compton Herbarium;
the *Claasens* and their guide, *Seroto Mohlala,* at the Echo Caves;
and finally, her daughter, *Barbara Evans,* who acted as her photographic assistant.

ISBN 0 86977 303 8

Contents

Title page: sunrise, looking eastwards over the Lowveld towards
the Lebombo Mountains in the far distance.
Overleaf: the Mount Sheba Hotel and guest cottages are within
a 1 500-hectare private nature reserve – a wonderland of
indigenous rain-forest sprawling along a valley watered by
tributaries of the Blyde River.

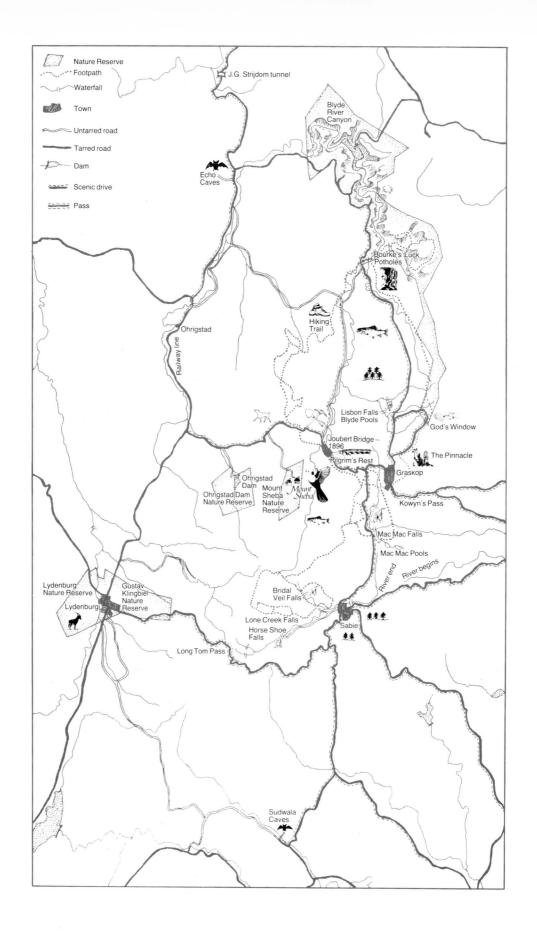

Nature Reserve
Footpath
Waterfall
Town
Untarred road
Tarred road
Dam
Scenic drive
Pass

J.G. Strijdom tunnel

Blyde
River
Canyon

Bourke's Luck
Potholes

Echo
Caves

Hiking
Trail

Ohrigstad

Lisbon Falls
Blyde Pools

God's Window

Joubert Bridge —
1896

The Pinnacle

Pilgrim's Rest

Graskop

Railway line

Ohrigstad
Dam

Mount
Sheba
Nature
Reserve

Mount
Sheba

Kowyn's Pass

Ohrigstad Dam
Nature Reserve

Mac Mac Falls

Mac Mac Pools

River end   River begins

Lydenburg
Nature Reserve

Gustav
Klingbiel
Nature
Reserve

Bridal
Veil Falls

Lydenburg

Lone Creek Falls

Sabie

Horse Shoe
Falls

Long Tom Pass

Sudwala
Caves

Foreword

I read *The Golden Escarpment* from cover to cover one evening while sitting in the warm kitchen of my small Karkloof farm in the midlands of Natal. The winter sun had disappeared behind the Drakensberg and the red-winged starlings had stopped calling. The book brought to the surface long-forgotten memories, when I was a boy of eight travelling to an uncle's farm, "Curlews", in the White River district. As a treat during the holidays my cousin and I would be taken to Pilgrim's Rest and Graskop and to Skukuza in the Kruger National Park. I remember the groves of orange trees shining in the winter sunlight and the morning mists on the long climb to Pilgrim's Rest. I remember too sitting around the open fire at Skukuza with the smell of acacia wood and the sound of lions roaring across the river. Later I read *Jock of the Bushveld* and my life was given an impetus which led to the conservation of nature becoming a passion and eventually a career.

The Golden Escarpment is an outstanding book, factual, very well written, with a warm understanding of a unique part of South Africa. It fills many gaps in the history of Pilgrim's Rest and gathers together much of the wonderful lore.

I was sad when I came to the end of the book and for days afterwards I found myself sighing or chuckling at some of the stories. Everyone will be able to identify with the romantic diggers who came from all over the world, seeking a fortune. The Celts in particular were pioneers in many parts of the world. I have seen their graves not only in Pilgrim's Rest but in Virginia City near Reno in the State of Nevada. Yet, as the author says, the mists and streams of the Drakensberg were so like the burns of Scotland and the hills of Wales that the similarity as well as the search for gold kept them in South Africa.

The tales of the patriarchal Trekker leaders and their quarrelsome followers as they bravely trekked with their wagons over the escarpment and across the deadly lowveld to Lourenço Marques will always be remembered in the history of South Africa.

Today South Africa is in a new era, with a different trek in process that will be as painful and as bloody and yet as glorious in the end as the trek our forefathers experienced. *The Golden Escarpment* is a milestone in the new trek because it shows us where we have come from and indicates that there is a new gold lode, not one beneath the earth of the Witwatersrand but one to be found in the hearts and souls of all South Africans, black, white, coloured and Indian, who will have to move into the new century only fourteen years away.

DR IAN PLAYER D.M.S.

Top left: one of the 'dolmens' of the region – rocky outcrops carved to a fantasia of shapes by wind and time. This one is called 'The Lost City'. *Left:* aloes reflected in the waters of Kearney's Creek. *Above:* evening shadows creep over The Lost City; clumps of aloes provide a counterpoint to the patterns of the rocks.

Mid-nineteenth century Lydenburg – the mis-named 'Town of Suffering' that became happy home to the earliest of the eastern Boer settlers – with its Voortrekker school and church in the foreground.

The beckoning land

A few years after the turn of the century, a curious case was heard in Lydenburg's courthouse. On trial was one Thomas Dennison, known to friends and creditors alike as Tommy. He was accused of holding up the Zeederberg mail-coach on the road between Lydenburg and Pilgrim's Rest, armed with a pair of carved wooden pistols of his own manufacture.

The robbery took place on the evening of 7 June, 1912. The coach, drawn by mules, was making its leisurely way through the pass at the crest of the long hill which runs down to the Blyde River and Pilgrim's Rest. It was at this point, thirteen years before, that there had been a notorious and successful highway robbery. Now, on this mild June evening, history appeared to be repeating itself. One of the passengers, Peter Williams, reported that a masked figure placed its foot on the back step of the carriage and levelled two pistols into it, one of them pointing directly at Williams's chest.

Then a strange voice, with an American accent, barked out instructions. They were all told to put up their hands, and the driver to throw out 'that box of gold you loaded up in Lydenburg this morning!' A moment later, the passengers heard a thud as something hit the ground. The robber hopped off the coach, and in the same curious voice ordered the driver on. He was last seen standing beside his booty, watching the coach as it rattled away into the dusk.

Two things had impressed the passengers: the highwayman's obviously faked accent, and the startling resemblance of its timbre to that of the well-known local character, Tommy Dennison. A cockney by birth, Dennison had come out to South Africa as a private in the British Army during the Anglo-Boer War. For a while he had been a dispatch rider to the Earl of Athlone. After the war, reluctant to go home, he had gravitated to Pilgrim's Rest. There he had worked as the village barber before becoming a kind of general laundryman to the unmarried men of the village. His cheerfully feckless character and an addiction to the Royal Hotel, however, had led him into debt. Memory of the earlier hold-up had prompted him to try his own luck.

In the event, it proved to be a small haul. Dennison got away, briefly, with £129 in silver and florins and half-crowns, but his common sense seemed to match the extent of his ill-gotten gains, for the day after the robbery he was seen in Pilgrim's Rest, frantically paying off his debts in coins. It wasn't long before he was tracked down and apprehended in the Royal Hotel, where he was busy drinking down the last of the loot. The court took him more seriously than he professed to take himself. He was found guilty as charged, and sent off for five years as a guest of the State in Pretoria Central Prison. With a year remitted from his sentence, he emerged unrepentant, his American accent intact. Returning to Pilgrim's Rest, he opened 'The Highwayman Garage'. The wooden pistols used in the robbery were defiantly nailed over the door for all to see and admire.

The hero of the last mail-coach robbery in South Africa, Dennison earned himself a small but secure place in the cast of local eccentrics. Even in his own day he was regarded as a human nugget; a character to be prized. Nor was he by any means the only one to leave a good story in the hills and valleys around Pilgrim's Rest. For this green and pleasant corner of the eastern Transvaal, the mountain region of the Drakensberg escarpment, has a history rich in personality and event.

It was here in the 1840s, for example, that a minor branch of the Great Trek came to a halt. Against heavy odds, the Trekkers broke the land, planted and harvested it. They founded settlements such as the ill-fated Andries-Ohrigstad, and Lydenburg which, despite its melancholy name – it means 'town of suffering' – was to flourish, briefly becoming a Trekker Republic in its own right. Of these early communities, little remains today but a handful of lovingly restored buildings.

But of a later development, much is still in evidence. For this was the region which saw South Africa's first historic gold-rush. It took place among the creeks and valleys of Mac Mac and Pilgrim's Rest, beginning as a trickle and becoming a flood. Into the tranquil world of the farmers, the diggers of the 1870s brought their new and raucous ways.

The mining community had its counterparts in the gold-rush towns of California and Australia and, nearer to home, in the diamond fields of Kimberley in the northern Cape. A rag-tag collection of men – diggers and chancers and drifters, and not a few individuals of real stature and ability – packed up their mostly meagre belongings to set out on the long, dusty and often dangerous journey to these distant valleys.

Abject poverty and sudden wealth existed side by side in the diggings. For the luckier ones, large nuggets glistened among the stones, 'tails' of gold in iron pans or in the 'Venetian ripples' of the prospectors' sluice-boxes. Fortunes were made and lost, but for the majority the rewards remained modest. A few men returned home, disappointed; many stayed to squander their hard-earned finds in the local bars, and to leave their bones in the hot little graveyard on the hill above Pilgrim's Rest. A sad number of them died without the few ounces of gold needed for a headstone.

In the 1880s, new and vastly greater discoveries were made on the Witwatersrand. These drew many of the shaggy hopefuls away from the Lydenburg fields. The deeper deposits and 'leaders' of gold, inaccessible to the lone prospector, were left to be developed later, by companies with more capital and better technical resources. By the early decades of the century, some £30 million-worth of gold had been dug from the earth around Pilgrim's Rest, but then the tide slowly retreated. The last of the mines, the famous Theta, was deproclaimed in the early 1970s. Now, only a handful of old-timers cling stubbornly to their claims, though many remember with poignant clarity the heady days of the past.

Since the deproclamation of the area, Pilgrim's Rest has become a museum town, faithfully representing the character of a typical nineteenth century mining community. Originally built as a temporary camp it has become, ironically, a permanent centre. The imported, prefabricated wooden shacks, with their red tin roofs, run parallel to Pilgrim's Creek, the stream that winds down the acacia-shaded valley, thirty metres below. The valley's slopes are pitted and scarred with the long decades of excavation. Piles of boulders are evidence of the rugged, sweat-filled labour that was needed simply to make enough money to stay alive. Many of the adits – the near-horizontal shafts – are gradually becoming overgrown with grass and bush. If the houses, with their Victorian furniture, pictures and bric-a-brac and their neat cottage gardens are one kind of monument, these man-made scars on the face of the land are another: a powerful reminder of the lure of gold, and of the ephemeral nature of dreams.

Left: the forlorn relics of one of the old Mount Sheba diggings, its entrance half-obscured by foliage and the creeping undergrowth of decades. A few of the early miners extracted modest fortunes from the excavations of the area; most lived, and left, in poverty. *Above:* the view from the interior of an adit, a shaft driven deep into the rock. The tunnel remains as a silent memorial to the anonymous diggers of the gold-rush era. *Below:* the 'Miner's Kitchen' at Mount Sheba – a rough but serviceable construction of stone built into the hillside.

Of the diggers' halcyon days, the modern visitor can see only relics. But there are other forms of wealth here, and they are all around. When it comes to natural beauty and variety, this must be one of the richest areas in southern Africa. From the meandering streams, the valley slopes rise up to high hills, tier upon tier, in great swelling configurations, patterned and caressed by the clear Highveld light. The highest mountains in the Transvaal, they culminate to the south-west of Pilgrim's Rest, in the 2 285 metre-high Mount Anderson. But the most impressive of the region's natural formations, one which gives the whole area its unique character, is the Drakensberg escarpment itself.

A thousand metres high on average, it runs in a north-south direction, stretching from the canyon of the Blyde River down to Kowyn's Pass and Graskop, and thence down again to Sabie.

This part of South Africa's Great Escarpment is a vast geological fault dividing the Highveld plateau to the west from the coastal plains of the Lowveld to the east. Each of these areas – plateau, escarpment and marginal zone – has its own character, climate and distinctive animal and plant life. Much of the Lowveld is now farmland, but some of its original personality can be seen in the Kruger National Park, which runs parallel to the escarpment along the eastern – the Mozambique – border of the Transvaal.

The escarpment was created, many millions of years ago, by a series of seismic upheavals on an unbelievably massive scale. Though the Transvaal heights bear the same name as Natal's range, and are an apparent continuation of the Natal 'Berg, their origins are different. The latter was formed by the collision of geological masses which thrust the strata upwards. The escarpment of the eastern Transvaal, on the other hand, was the product of counter-pressure on the Highveld plateau to the west. Here the first level to be laid down, about 2 000 million years ago, was archean granite. Over this were deposited alternating layers of shale and quartzite, the latter eroding more slowly than the softer shale. On top of these a stratum of dolomite was laid down, followed by further levels of shale and quartzite.

This colossal layer-cake of rock was then violently disturbed by volcanic eruptions from below. Under great pressure, vast quantities of molten igneous rock were driven up through the granite crust. They settled and spread as a further layer of the region of what is now called the Springbok Flats. In many areas of the escarpment, fragments of this ancient laval matter, some of the oldest rocks known on earth, can be seen as 'volcanic bombs' – scatters of giant boulders – deposited on the hillsides. On the Highveld, the lava reached so great a mass as to fracture and crush the strata below. In doing so, it forced the outer edges of the great bowl of land upwards, creating a huge escarpment, characterized by many rifts and faults. Among this chaotic tangle of geological series were the ore-bearing rocks which contained the 'ash-blond' gold of the miners' dreams.

The scale on which this primordial upheaval took place is evident throughout the mountain region, but especially in the series of 'ledges' that step down from the heights above Pilgrim's Rest. From Lydenburg, one can follow the road to Robbers' Pass at the crest of the plateau. From there the way descends, following the old coach and wagon route, to the valley of the Blyde River, then rises again to the rim of the wide valley of Graskop. Here, on the descent, can be seen the first of the towering cliffs, girt with thick forests at foot and crest. Across the valley, the road runs on to the village of Graskop, and to the rim of the next and even grander series of cliffs. The view from God's Window, a few kilometres from the village of Graskop, looks out over one of the country's most majestic vistas. Far below, a thickly-woven green carpet of state-owned forests rolls away into the hazy distance, to the Lowveld proper and to the far horizon of the Lebombo Mountains.

The Voortrekkers came from the Highveld and established their villages and farms on the high ground. Others, though, came from the east, across the Lowveld plain. Today, the land sleeps quietly enough in the sun, but in the early days such a journey was not lightly undertaken. The region was a baking wilderness of sand, scrub and fever-trees, of rivers and swamps, predatory animals and, above all, of malaria and tsetse fly. The way through it was long and hard, and it was perilously easy to become lost. Many and blood-chilling are the tales of these hazards of the Lowveld. Nowhere, though, has its character, its dangers and the perverse fascination it had for men of the road been better captured than in Percy FitzPatrick's classic book, *Jock of the Bushveld*.

In his early twenties, the adventure-hungry FitzPatrick became a transport-rider, a breed that flourished and created its own legends in the heyday of the goldfields. They drove their supply-laden wagons from the port of Lourenço Marques (now Maputo), in what was then Portuguese East Africa, across the Komati and Crocodile rivers to the settlements of Mac Mac and Pilgrim's Rest. The journey had to be made in a hundred days or not at all, since this was the period from the bite of the tsetse fly to the point where a trek-ox would begin to die from the disease carried by the insect. And if 'the fly' did not sabotage the venture, there were still the lions that circled just beyond the flickering light of the camp fire, waiting to carry off an unprotected ox, and the vultures and hyenas that cleaned the remains. Hunting supplied the pot, but many a man failed to return from a foray. The risk of fever disappeared at the foothills of the 'Berg, but the journey was far from over. Ahead lay the steep wagon-trail up the face of the escarpment. On the more formidable inclines teams of up to eighty oxen were attached to a single wagon. The way ran along the ridges of the hills to the mining-camps, which were always anxious, sometimes desperate for the food, whisky and gin and much-needed equipment that had been delivered, often at tragic cost.

After the sultry heat of the sub-tropical Lowveld, the uplands air was clear, cool and healthy, though it tended, in the winter months, to thicken to clammy mist. The transport-rider could earn good money, and at the end of his journey there would be spirited celebrations in the canteens of Pilgrim's Rest and Mac Mac. Soon afterwards the lightened wagons would rattle away, back down the slopes and across the plains to the port and a fresh load.

In FitzPatrick, as in many of the miners themselves, there was a strong streak of the poet and the romantic. For all their hunger for fortune, they came to love the country, its great quiet spaces and its dignity. The Scotsmen and Welshmen among them – and there were many Celts in the goldfields, as a visit to their graveyards will testify – saw echoes of the hills of home, not least in the many upland streams and rivers that work their way down the escarpment, bearing their tantalizing glint of gold from the rocks through which they have passed. In the catchment area, a myriad small water courses feed rivers such as the Blyde, the Treur, the Letaba, the Steelpoort and the Spekboom, all of which in turn lead into the Olifants River. The Olifants emerges from the region to the north, joining the Limpopo on its course to the sea. South of Lydenburg, the Crocodile and Komati rivers also wind their way to the sea, but farther south, near Maputo.

In their mountain setting, these rivers are laced by quiet pools – their fresh, chill waters are often the haunt of trout – and by a great number of waterfalls. Indeed, the escarpment of the Transvaal Drakensberg can provide almost a reference book on the variety and delights of the waterfall. Some tumble down the open mountainside, others are hidden away in the cool and secret depths of the forests. They range from the Sabie Falls through the Lisbon and Berlin falls, to perhaps the most spectacular of all, the magnificent double waterfall of Mac Mac, plummeting a dizzying 65 metres into the shadowed gorge below. Around almost every waterfall a mantle of mosses, ferns and ancient cycads clothes the area of the splash zone. Dense growths of indigenous trees and bush cluster around and overhang the cascades, their undergrowth alive with an infinity of small birds, animals and insects.

Each of these rivers has made its own contribution to the story of erosion. This reaches its most dramatic manifestation on the northern edge of the escarpment, in the canyon worn out over countless millions of years by the Blyde River, a tributary of the Olifants. In its early reaches, the river runs modestly enough under the bridge leading to Pilgrim's Rest, and then meanders at its own gentle pace northwards. The Blyde's way goes through a broad valley, where its alluvial deposits have left good farming land. For twenty kilometres, a dirt road follows the course of the river, crossing and recrossing it. Then, abruptly, as the river approaches the rim of the escarpment, the character and mood of the landscape change. The valley opens into a wide basin, and the river plunges into a deep, narrow gorge.

It is at this point – from one of the vertigo-inducing bridges that span the gorge – that one can view the sculptured wonders of the Bourke's Luck potholes. Tom Bourke was an early, and lucky, prospector who owned a claim nearby. The complex of holes to which he gave his name is a product of erosion at its most extraordinary, worn from the rock strata over aeons of time by the circular motion of the river's swirls and eddies to create a fantasia of ornamental shapes. The walls of the gorge, too, have been transformed in similar rococo fashion, scooped and scalloped, smoothed and polished, the patterns enriched by the different colours of the rock layers.

After this curtain-raiser comes the drama of the main section of the gorge. The road curves around its western edge, offering a series of stunning views, both into the canyon and beyond, through great gaps in the formations, to the blue-grey plain of the Lowveld. So awesome is the vista that it requires almost an effort of will to gaze down the eight hundred metres and millions of years of rock strata reaching to the rippling river below, its soft roar resonating in the cavernous grandeur of this 'chasm measureless to man'. Faraway across the void, massive broken buttresses and battlements of rock culminate in the 'Three Rondavels', a homely name for geological bastions magnificent in their stark immensity.

The power of water as an agent of erosion, visible to all on the surface, has its more secretive counterpart underground.

The convulsions of geological evolution led to a complex pattern of hard and soft rock formations in which are found many caverns. To the north of Andries-Ohrigstad, for example, are the Echo Caves. But of all those in the region, or indeed in South Africa, perhaps the most impressive are the Sudwala Caves, a few kilometres to the west of Nelspruit. Discovered over a century ago, they had long been a place of refuge for tribes in time of war, and many relics of their occupation, in the shapes of bones and pot fragments, have been found. A series of caverns, one of them an incredible forty metres high, is connected by winding passageways running five kilometres into the mountain. Across millions of years, seepage from above, through the line of fault, has eroded the rock, baring the convolutions of the mineral strata. It has also generated a strange cast of stone creatures: stalactites and stalagmites of wonderful complexity and variety.

After these cavernous splendours one emerges into the sunshine to contemplate with equal pleasure man's part in the creation of this landscape. In the valleys maize and tobacco grow; sheep and cattle graze the pleasant uplands. But perhaps most eye-catching are the famed peach trees which grace the countryside with their vivid springtime colours. No one is quite certain how they came to be here, for they are not indigenous. The most persuasive theory is that they were planted, inadvertently, by early hunters and explorers. Along with the mandatory biltong, these intrepid men carried dried peaches, a favourite item. The pips, casually tossed aside, germinated and the trees grew to mark the paths of their wanderings. Now the trees contribute to the local produce. As well as the 'wild' ones, there are many cultivated orchards, yielding fine large yellow peaches.

If the peaches began as a happy accident, many of the other species in the region appeared by design. Despite the barely average soil fertility, trees thrive. The escarpment is well-watered, for it is a natural rain-trap. Rain, supplemented by the condensation of thick mists, delivers up to 1 000 millimetres a year.

Once, this moisture supported dense indigenous woods, all but impenetrable. Now almost all the escarpment and much of the adjacent Lowveld is covered by huge state-owned forests – they are, in fact, the largest man-made woodlands in the world. Species include pines, yellowwoods and gum-trees. Most of the timber finds its way into the paper industry or to the mines of the Witwatersrand. These forests have transformed the original character of the land. Regrettably, too, they have led to a decline in animal and bird life. Pines in particular plunder the soil's nutrition, and few other plants are capable of surviving beneath them.

But in many places the earlier vegetation survives. The wilder uplands, beyond man's reach, are covered with scrub and aloes. The hills around Andries-Ohrigstad, for example, still have an untouched look, and in a number of other areas the flora is officially protected. The Blyde River Canyon is a nature reserve, as are the areas around the Ohrigstad Dam and Mount Sheba. One of the most impressive of the region's reserves lies a few kilometres to the west of Pilgrim's Rest, at Mount Sheba. Here, some 1 500 hectares of indigenous rain forest sprawling along a valley and watered by a number of streams leading down to the Blyde River, have been set aside as a private nature reserve. An impressive number and variety of indigenous tree species have been recorded in the land around the river, ranging from such well-known varieties as yellowwood to unusual and often exotically named species such as wild peach, cabbage tree, silky bark, wild lemon, bastard onionwood, notsung, poison olive, black ironwood, and bachelor's refuge, the last-named having smooth, curved branches rising up beyond a maiden's presumed reach. Here, too, and especially around the farthest waterfalls, are many ferns, conifers and cycads, inhabitants of the earth before the advent of flowering plants and deciduous trees.

This is ancient Africa, as it was for millennia before the coming of man. When precisely he did arrive on the escarpment is not known. Traces of the area's aboriginal inhabitants – the Bushmen – have been found in many of the local caves and rock shelters, most with clear views over land that once teemed with game, and which often harboured enemies. Skilful hunters, these Stone Age people fashioned weapons and implements from bone and flint, of which remains have been unearthed and studied by archaeologists.

Then, about 2 000 years ago, tall, Bantu-speaking Nguni people moved down in successive waves from central Africa, displacing the Bushmen. They settled in a broad band across the Transvaal Highveld, the mountains of the escarpment, and the Lowveld. Unlike their Khoisan predecessors, the newcomers mined and worked metal, principally iron and copper. There is evidence that they also used local gold, if only for ornament. They made their homes both in caves and in the open, in settled villages of 'wattle and daub' huts, usually along the river banks. Though they were adept as hunters, they also practised simple agriculture, keeping sheep, goats and cattle, and planting crops.

Ample evidence of these Iron Age people has been found in upwards of fifty mountain cave sites. One particular archaeological treasure-hunt, at the so-called 'Head Site' outside Lydenburg, yielded an intriguing collection of relics. Carbon-dated to about 500 AD, they included a large cache of pottery shards which, when restored, were revealed as clay masks. There were seven of them: six of human faces, one of an animal face. Probably used in religious or initiation ceremonies, they are decorated with ritual scars, have slits for eyes and mouths, the features topped by stylized hair patterns and embellished with small animal figures. Though the originals are kept in the South African Museum in Cape Town, copies of these mysterious, sinister-looking artefacts are on display at Lydenburg's museum, together with representations of the excavations themselves.

By the fifteenth century, the Bantu-speakers were firmly entrenched as far south as the fringes of the eastern Cape into which the Khoisan had retreated. Split into families, clans and tribes, their common origin and similar language did not deter them from waging more or less constant warfare against one another. This, at least, was the impression gained by the first Europeans to venture among them.

These were the Portuguese navigators and explorers who, from the middle of the fifteenth century, had begun to creep down the western coast of the continent. The process had culminated in the closing years of the century with the epic voyages of Bartolomeu Dias and Vasco da Gama. Dias was the first to round the tip of Africa; Da Gama charted the sea-route to India and the Spice Islands, giving powerful impetus to trade between Europe and the Orient, a trade that would flourish for four centuries.

The Portuguese mariners came ashore to take on water and to barter for meat and other provisions with the local tribes – with the Hottentot and Bushman clans of the Khoisan in the south, and the Nguni on the eastern seaboard. It was in the latter region that, in due course, they established a permanent base. Delagoa Bay was an isolated, swamp- and river-enclosed port settlement of palisaded fort and mud-brick buildings, and it was destined to play an indirect but significant rôle in the story of the future Transvaal. The last stop on the way to India, its main function was to serve as a repair, maintenance and revictualling depot for the Portuguese trading fleet.

The Portuguese did explore the interior, tentatively, and indulged in some modest inland trading. But the Lowveld was approached with understandable caution, though later on more intrepid hunters and traders took their chances with lions, crocodiles and fever to traffic in hides, ivory and slaves – items which were often the booty from local tribal clashes. But the limit of Portuguese penetration was clearly delineated. The brooding face of the granite and shale escarpment that ended the Lowveld plain was a forbidding obstacle. Thus it was that the mysterious land beyond the mountains – the escarpment and the Highveld – was left to others to explore and settle. The presence of the Portuguese at Delagoa Bay, however, was to be a major incentive to this process.

The arrival of the Voortrekkers at the escarpment in the mid-1830s was the climax of a long and complex series of events. The story began almost two centuries before, when the great Dutch trading enterprise, the Dutch East-India Company, established a small settlement at the Cape of Good Hope. Its purpose was similar to that of Delagoa Bay: it was to be a repair and revictualling station for the Company's fleet, plying between Holland and the Dutch possessions in the Islands of Spice, which they called Batavia. With this in mind, the Company's directors, in 1652, dispatched one of its officials, a certain Jan van Riebeeck, together with some hundred men and a handful of women and children to the southern extremity of the African continent.

The original brief from the directors – the Lords Seventeen – specified limited objectives: there was no question in their minds of founding a permanent colony on the Peninsula, let alone of settling the entire Cape. Yet as early as Van Riebeeck's short tenure the first 'Free Burgher' farmers were released from the Company's service to cultivate their own land. In time, these men came to form the nucleus of a new settler society, a community of Protestant Dutch-speaking farmers occupying the southern rim of Africa. While they retained much that reflected their Dutch origins – their language, customs and religion – other features of their society were special to their African situation. Among these was a dependence upon slave labour. The slaves were a mixed population, drawn from the Dutch conquests in the east, from Portuguese territory in Africa, and from the local Hottentot and Bushman peoples.

During the eighteenth century, the frontier farmers spread inland and along the coastal belt to the east. It was here, from about the middle of the century onwards, that they came in contact and conflict with the southernmost, Xhosa-speaking black people. Skirmishes escalated into full-scale confrontations. Altogether nine frontier wars were fought during the latter part of the eighteenth and in the nineteenth century.

With the decline of the Dutch East-India Company, the farmers of the Cape gained a large measure of independence – a liberty they came to value passionately, and which they were to lose when a new administration came to govern at the Cape. For a number of reasons connected with the French Revolutionary and Napoleonic wars, the British invaded the colony in July 1795. A British Military Governor was installed in the Castle at Table Bay. Seven years later, with the Treaty of Amiens (which formalized a state of 'armed neutrality'), the colony was handed back to the interim Dutch Batavian Republican government, but then, with the renewal of hostilities in Europe in 1806, the invaders returned – and this time they stayed.

The Dutch settlers, especially those in the rugged eastern border areas, deeply resented the new authority, but were powerless to act. In fact they did, eventually, take up arms, but the Slagter's Nek Rebellion of 1815 was brief, and easily suppressed. Thereafter, for two acrimonious decades, the pot of discontent simmered, needing just one more ingredient before it had to boil over. The British duly added this, in December 1835, when they proclaimed the formal emancipation of all slaves in their dominions.

Abolition of slavery was not, perhaps, the most bitterly felt of the Boers' grievances, but it was the last item in a long litany of irritation that included bureaucratic interference in local community affairs, over-taxation, an alien and autocratic educational policy and, above all, the failure of the British regime to halt Xhosa raids and stock thefts.

There was angry debate in the hills and valleys, crystallizing in a common impulse. Mass migration, it was held, was the only practical defence against the assault on Boer independence.

Thus began the Great Trek, one of the momentous events of South African history. About half the farming population of the colony, some 5 000 people, sold their property, loaded their wives and children into ox-wagons, and set out in a number of parties and groups for the great unknown beyond the Orange River, which was then the northern boundary of the Cape. Within two decades, and against enormous odds, they were to establish three Voortrekker Republics: the Orange Free State, the Transvaal and the Republic of Natalia. Of these, the first two were to survive, and then only with great difficulty.

Among the areas that eventually came to be settled was the eastern Transvaal. The story is one of complexity and of many setbacks, largely caused, it must be said, by the almost compulsively quarrelsome nature of the Voortrekker leaders. But these men did play the essential rôle in opening up the interior. They included Andries Hendrik Potgieter and his arch-rival, Andries Pretorius. However, the first to make his way into the rolling hills and valleys of the Transvaal Drakensberg was Louis Trichardt. His pioneering expedition was to prove epic in length, and tragic in its outcome.

The pathfinders

Trichardt's plan was simple enough; its execution a lot less so. He intended to find an area for settlement which, besides offering fertile land, would also have access to a port. However, there were few good natural harbours on the eastern seaboard. One was already well-known: the Port of Natal, on the shores of Zulu country. By the start of the Great Trek, though, it was already held by a group of English traders and hunters. And British ambitions for Natal as a whole were already clear. The only other port was that of Delagoa Bay. But it was still more remote, and in Portuguese-held territory.

The Trekker leaders were divided over the issue. Trichardt regarded it as axiomatic that freedom could be achieved only out of range of British influence, and he ruled out Natal. Others concurred, among them Johannes van Rensburg. He and Trichardt agreed to join forces to locate new land and to establish trading contacts with Delagoa Bay.

Before they left, they made a pact with another of the leaders, a man who was later to have a powerful influence on the course of events in the future Transvaal Republic – Andries Hendrik Potgieter. Tall and gaunt, autocratic by temperament and possessed of a restless, fiercely questing spirit, Potgieter was in his early forties at the time of the Great Trek. He had grown up on the family farm in the Graaff-Reinet district of the Cape and, as a young man, had taken part in the Fourth and Fifth Frontier Wars, gaining excellent experience for the challenges that lay ahead. As one of the 'border boers' of the Cape Colony he had bitterly resented paying taxes to a British administration that had failed to provide protection from the Xhosa. As a consequence he had an abiding compulsion to escape from British-ruled territory and, at the start of the Trek, readily agreed to throw in his lot with Trichardt. On the eve of departure, however, more frontier trouble broke out and he was delayed. He promised to join Trichardt in the north at a later date.

Trichardt and Van Rensburg each led a party of nine wagons, taking with them several thousand head of cattle. They crossed the Cape border at the Orange River, then continued north across the land which was to become the Orange Free State. In April 1836 they reached the Vaal River, which they forded at the Elandspruit confluence. They were now in new and wild territory, little known except to a handful of missionaries, and the occasional, solitary trekboer.

The two parties separated north of the Vaal. Van Rensburg and his people went ahead, to allow time for the grazing to recover behind them. They followed the western edge of the Drakensberg range, finally outspanning at the Soutpansberg, in the country of the Venda people, some 200 kilometres north of the Drakensberg escarpment. But Van Rensburg was impatient to find a way to the sea, so rather than wait for Trichardt to catch up he pushed ahead, into the Bushveld to the east. When Trichardt arrived a few weeks later he found the Soutpansberg camp deserted. His party outspanned in the southern lee of the mountain, rested their cattle, erected makeshift shelters, and planted wheat and corn. Whatever time they had left after these chores they filled with their favourite pastime: arguing among themselves about the next move.

The Sixth Frontier War concluded, Hendrik Potgieter left his farm two months after the main party. With him were about thirty men together with their wives, children and servants. In the region of today's Winburg, in the Orange Free State, they made their first stop. A local chieftain, in return for a small herd of cattle and protection against his enemies, ceded the Trekkers all the land between the Vet and Vaal rivers, and for many of the party this seemed sufficient of an earthly paradise. They decided to settle where they were.

But the ever-restless Potgieter moved on to keep his rendezvous with Trichardt. Joined by eleven other men and their families, he followed the trail to the camp under the Soutpansberg, where he learned of Van Rensburg's disappearance into the thorn-brake two months before.

They were not to know that Van Rensburg and his entire party had already met their fate. Journeying to the east through ever more hostile territory, controlled by a chieftain named Soshangane, they had encamped beside the Limpopo, on the far side of the Lebombo range. Here, in a surprise attack, Soshangane's warriors annihilated the group.

Despite the rumours of disaster that were filtering in, Trichardt decided on a search party. He was joined by a number of Van Rensburg's relatives who had arrived with Potgieter. With some trepidation, they set off to the east.

Meanwhile, Potgieter departed on a private exploration to the north, penetrating over a hundred kilometres beyond the Limpopo, into today's Zimbabwe, where there was good grazing land and a fine climate. But the region was remote from the sea, and he retraced his steps. By the time he arrived back at the Soutpansberg, Trichardt, too, had returned. The search party had found no living trace of Van Rensburg and his people, though weapons, utensils and pieces of Trekker clothing were seen with ominous frequency in the hands of the local tribesmen. Unnerved by the air of hostility sensed in the lawless land around them, they had turned back.

Potgieter told Trichardt of his journey to the north. Despite its distance from the sea, he felt this was promising land. He undertook to return to Winburg, and to bring back the main body of his followers. In August, he took his leave of Trichardt and rode away to the south.

Alone again, Trichardt and his group debated the possible fate of Van Rensburg. A number of Trekkers, led by Jan Pretorius, insisted on a second and more thorough search. Reluctantly Trichardt agreed, but he himself remained behind to hold the camp. Pretorius and three other men, together with their womenfolk, inspanned four of the wagons and set off on the second expedition.

While they were gone, Trichardt's mind turned to the real purpose of the journey, which was to make contact with the Portuguese Governor at the fort and settlement at Delagoa Bay – Lourenço Marques – with a view to establishing trading links. By now the Trekkers were running low on food and essential items, including coffee. This latter was a major deprivation since the average Boer would endure almost any hardship rather than go without his pot of scalding black brew morning and evening.

Then, early in 1837, a party of African pedlars arrived at the camp. They were returning from the hinterland to their base on the coast, and they suggested to Trichardt that he should sound out the Portuguese Governor by letter. Accordingly, on 11 May, 1837, Trichardt sat down to pen a carefully worded missive to 'The Honourable Gentlemen and Friends at Delagoa Bay' outlining his party's situation and plans and offering to supply the Portuguese with cattle, sheep, wool, ox-hides and the skins of 'wild beasts'. He also appended, on behalf of his wife Martha, a dignified plea for supplies of tea and coffee.

It was simple enough to commit his thoughts to paper, quite another matter to have the letter delivered. Lourenço Marques was far away, the route uncharted and hazardous. But here Trichardt had a stroke of luck, in the amiable shape of one Gabriel de Buys, son of Coenraad, an adventurous soul who had left the Cape some years before for the solitude of the northern reaches of the subcontinent, eventually settling in the Soutspansberg region. Here he lived by the rewards of the hunt, and had produced a small tribe of mixed-race children, of whom Gabriel was one.

Gabriel offered to act as postman, managed to find his way to Lourenço Marques, and in due course two soldiers from the fort arrived at Trichardt's camp with a favourable response from the Portuguese Governor, Antonio Gamitto.

Meanwhile, after five long months of fruitless search, Pretorius's party had limped back to the camp. By now it was clear that Van Rensburg's chances of having survived were remote, and it was time they looked to their own welfare. With the assurance of Gamitto's letter, they broke camp and began their journey to the coast.

Trichardt chose a southerly route to the sea, via the Sabie River, rather than follow in Van Rensburg's tragic footsteps. For six weeks the expedition trundled uneventfully southwards over the Transvaal plain and then, towards the end of September 1837, they reached the southern edge of the Strydpoort Mountains. A week later they outspanned on the banks of a river where elephants were much in evidence, and they duly named it the Olifants River.

Beyond this rough and treacherous watercourse the mountain barrier to the Lowveld loomed large and apparently impenetrable. In some desperation Trichardt sent word to the local chief, Sekwati, who eventually arrived in person, bearing fine ivory and a calabash of heady marula beer – and a gloomy account of the tribulations the white men would face on their journey to the coast.

For the next five months the Trekkers were to perform heroic feats of stamina and improvisation under almost impossible conditions – all to the accompaniment of less-than-heroic internal discord. They began their epic trek by continuing along the northern bank of the Olifants River, then turning up the Matabata, one of its tributaries. Here, there was angry argument about the precise route to follow. Sekwati had described the traditional path up and over the mountains, but some of Trichardt's party pointed out that where a man might walk wagons may not necessarily follow, and urged that the expedition keep to the course of the river. Outnumbered and out-talked, Trichardt agreed to try the river route, and the wagons turned back to the Olifants. During the next five days the party was forced to ford the river – a hazardous undertaking at best – no less than thirteen times.

Trouble heaped upon trouble. The horses, it was discovered, were being bitten by flies – an ominous signal. There was further, bitter, argument: for four days the Trekkers acrimoniously debated the options. In the end Trichardt, thoroughly disillusioned, loaded up his wagon, inspanned, returned to the old camp, and then set out to find a way over the mountain heights. In due course the rest of his party, chagrined after their own unsuccessful efforts, rejoined him. Incredibly, the reunited group managed to manhandle their wagons up the steep and jagged slopes and, at the end of November, cold, wet, tired and miserable, they pulled up at the edge of the escarpment.

But now there was the daunting task of finding a way down the almost sheer face of the escarpment. While argument raged once more, the women did a little exploration on their own account, and came back with a sensible suggestion for a way down, provided, as they ironically put it, the men didn't mind a little hard work.

For the next two months, day after day, the Trekkers laboured to bring their wagons down a thousand metres of hair-raising gradients, watched all the while from below by the Lowveld tribespeople. Their eventual and triumphant arrival on level ground was celebrated with much festivity, and the oxen were outspanned and rested for a few days.

By now some of their animals had started to disappear, spirited away by local cattle-thieves, so Trichardt rounded up a group of hostages before setting out on the final stage of the journey to the east.

They had survived many perils, but there were still others ahead. As they penetrated deeper into the Lowveld, the party and their animals suffered grievously from tsetse fly and mosquitoes. Near the Sand River, they found ticks on the horses and cattle. At night, lions prowled the darkness around the camp, shattered the stillness with their roaring and carried off much of the stock. But the Trekkers persevered, and during the first week of March 1838, they reached the low-lying Lebombo range. This they crossed without incident, though Trichardt himself was laid low with malaria for a few days. He appeared to recover, however, and soon the wagons were moving into Portuguese territory. Here, the main obstacles to progress were treacherous swampland and crocodile-filled rivers.

Finally, at about three o'clock in the afternoon of Friday 13 April, they came in sight of the fort of Lourenço Marques, with the sea beckoning in the distance. As the wagons creaked to a halt under the acacia trees, the Trekkers fired off their guns in jubilation, and in gratitude for their safe deliverance from the perils of Highveld and Lowveld alike.

They were welcomed, a little warily, by the Governor – he deprived the men of their guns before allowing them into the fort. In the evening, though, Trichardt was entertained to tea, cakes and amiable talk on the subject of trade by Gamitto and his wife. The next day the guns were returned.

The object of the expedition had been accomplished. But it now became grimly clear that the celebrations were premature. The cattle were going down with sickness, and it was not long before malaria began to take its devastating toll of the men, women and children. Fever swept through the camp, and although the Governor did everything in his power to help, the death-rate soared. On 1 May, Trichardt lost his beloved wife Martha, recording her death in a last, poignant entry in his journal. A few days later he followed her.

It was a tragic end to a courageous and potentially rewarding venture. Of the 53 people in the group, only 26 survived. In due course they were shipped down the coast to Natal. It was to be many months before news of Trichardt's fate reached the outside world.

Meanwhile, life had been anything but dull for Hendrik Potgieter. His intention on his return from the Soutpansberg to the main Voortrekker base at Winburg was to gather his followers and rejoin Trichardt. Instead, it would be two full years before he was free to return north again, years spent in a series of punitive raids against the Matabele, a new and powerful force led by the renowned Mzilikazi.

The years before the Great Trek saw the eruption and tragic conclusion of what is known as the *Difaqane* – a cataclysmic convulsion among the Black peoples of the subcontinent that left countless thousands of corpses on the plains of the interior.

In essence, the *Difaqane* was a violent mass-migration of tribal groupings triggered by the territorial ambitions of the Zulu military genius Shaka. The illegitimate son of a minor chieftain, Shaka had risen to power in the first years of the nineteenth century through a combination of political acumen and ruthlessness, taking over and refining, in the 1820s, the efficient war machine created by his predecessor, Dingiswayo. This, in a series of lightning campaigns, displaced a number of neighbouring tribes, which moved on, in turn disrupting and sometimes destroying other communities. Mzilikazi, a member of the small Khumalo tribe, had served as one of Shaka's abler generals, and was then appointed commander of a Zulu raiding impi. In this capacity, Shaka sent him into the Transvaal to loot the Sotho kraals. This task duly performed, Mzilikazi made a risk-laden mistake: he kept some of the proceeds for himself and refused to report back to Shaka, defiantly remaining in the mountains. Furious, the Zulu king dispatched a punitive force, which crept up on Mzilikazi's camp at night and killed most of the rebels. At dawn, Mzilikazi and 300 survivors withdrew in some haste to the north. Thereafter, he carved a bloody path across the plains of the Transvaal, pillaging, massacring some who stood in his way, absorbing others after defeating them, so that the fledgling Matabele kingdom grew strong in capability and in numbers.

In 1828 Shaka was murdered by his half-brother, Dingane, but the pattern of violence continued. The new king saw no reason to change his predecessor's vengeful policy towards Mzilikazi, and sent an army through the Drakensberg. Warned of the impending attack, Mzilikazi retreated northwards, settling in a new capital situated in a bowl of hills — the site of today's Pretoria. Here, in July 1832, the Zulu impis finally caught up with him. The Matabele army was cut to pieces, and again Mzilikazi fled, this time to the remote Marico area of the western Transvaal. It was here, at Mosega, that he established his third capital, and it was from here, in August 1836, that he launched his first onslaught against the Voortrekkers.

Stephanus Erasmus and his party of eight hunters was an isolated little group independent of the main body of the Trek. One day, at the end of a hunting expedition north of the Vaal River, they returned to their camp at Koppieskraal to find it occupied by 600 Matabele warriors, so they hurried off to the camp of a group of Trekkers, led by Barend Liebenberg, on the banks of the Vaal. Erasmus warned them of the danger, then rode on. The Liebenberg party was still assembling its laager when Mzilikazi's men descended on it. A tiny handful of Trekkers survived.

For Hendrik Potgieter, recently returned from the Soutpansberg, this was tantamount to a declaration of war and, helped by Sarel Cilliers, he assembled a punitive commando of 35 men. Their laager of 50 wagons, set on a hill soon to be named the Vechtkop or 'Battle Hill', drew Mzilikazi and some 3 000 of his soldiers, and battle was joined. The outcome, decisive from the strictly military point of view, was not all that the Trekkers could have wished. True, the impis were repulsed with heavy losses, but they did succeed in driving away the bulk of the Trekkers' livestock including 5 000 cattle and 50 000 sheep – an almost catastrophic loss. So, early in the following year Potgieter, now elevated to Commandant-General, set out with a force of over a hundred men. They crossed the Vaal at Kommandodrif, then rode north to Mzilikazi's capital in the basin of Mosega.

The Matabele were caught completely unprepared. Before dawn, the Trekkers attacked in a pincer movement, riding into the basin from two directions. Four hundred warriors were mown down with elephant guns loaded with shot, while the rest fled into the bush. The white men then made a thorough job of burning the kraals, retrieved their lost wagons and rounded up 7 000 head of cattle. The score had been more than evened.

In July, a Zulu raid further weakened Mzilikazi and, before he could recover, the Voortrekkers returned to inflict the *coup de grâce*. They were jointly led by Potgieter and Pieter Uys, and spent the day of 4 November, 1837 destroying Mzilikazi's capital. The main battle was fought the next day. Mzilikazi himself led his army against a line of 360 Trekkers supported by a force of Baro-

long and mixed-race Griqua soldiers. Two thousand Matabele died in the rout that followed. The shattered remnants fled into the deserts of Botswana. From there, Mzilikazi led them into the lands beyond the Limpopo where in present-day Zimbabwe the Matabele found their last and enduring home.

For the Voortrekkers, their bloody and successful campaign was a watershed event. By the end of 1837 the Transvaal had been secured for settlement, and Potgieter passionately urged the formal establishment of a new country beyond the Vaal. It was now, though, that he came up against powerful political opposition – from another legendary Trek leader, Andries Pretorius.

If a shade less zealous than Potgieter, Pretorius was as stubborn in his views. For him the Promised Land lay not to the north, but to the east. He had sent scouts through the main Drakensberg range. They had returned with glowing reports of green hills and fertile earth. But to Potgieter, there were obvious drawbacks to the option. The English, albeit tenuously, did hold the Port of Natal, and the region as a whole was the domain of Dingane, a tyrant who had preserved intact Shaka's empire and army and its uniquely effective fighting methods. Potgieter dourly predicted that the price for all this fine land would be war both with the British and with the Zulu.

Events were to prove Potgieter right, and Pretorius, for all his vision and acumen, sadly wrong. But at this moment the majority of Trekkers were against Potgieter, and he had to watch the wagons turn east through the Drakensberg. Soon enough one of his predictions had been brutally fulfilled.

As the Voortrekkers moved down into Natal, one of their leaders, Piet Retief, went ahead to parley with the Zulu king. With him were fifteen men, including his young son. After receiving Dingane's mark on a treaty ceding land for white settlement, a second meeting was held on 6 February, 1838, but in the midst of the proceedings the Trekker party was seized and dragged away to be murdered on kwaMatiwane, the Hill of Execution, close to the royal kraal. The massacre prompted the rest of the Natal Trekkers to send out frantic pleas for help.

With Uys, Potgieter went to their aid, only to be defeated at the Battle of Italeni on 10 April. Uys and his son, Dirkie, were killed, and Potgieter, accused of cowardice, was blamed for the disaster.

Potgieter withdrew, bitter and angry, to the Transvaal, and to his long-delayed meeting with Trichardt. But when he arrived at the old camp in the Soutpansberg he found only a few fields running to weed and a forlorn group of abandoned shacks. Reluctantly, he moved back south, with a new plan forming in his mind. He gathered up his remaining followers, crossed the Vaal and moved with them to the banks of the Mooi River, some 200 kilometres north of Winburg. Here he started the small settlement of Mooiriviersdorp. Unfortunately, the site was chosen in the dry season, and with the coming of the winter rains the villagers were flooded out. Abandoning Mooiriviersdorp, they moved ten kilometres farther up the river where they laid out a new town, which they named Potchefstroom – literally, 'Chief Potgieter's Stream'.

While all this was going on, matters were approaching a climax in Natal. Sunday 16 December, 1838, brought the decisive clash between Trekker and Zulu. The Battle of Blood River broke the power of Dingane's army, and opened the way – or so it seemed at the time – for Trekker settlement. With the king and his impis in full retreat and the royal kraal at Gungundlovu in flames, the wagons began to roll back into Natal.

There were thus two Voortrekker communities at this time, one on each side of the Drakensberg range, and the rivalry between Potgieter and Pretorius took a new turn, for the latter harboured ambitions to lead a unified state – one in which the Transvaal would be absorbed into the Natal Republic. But Potgieter was not about to lose his hard-won independence so easily – he was master of all he surveyed in the plains across the Vaal, and intended to remain so. He did, however, agree to a conference with Pretorius. This led to the formation of a Transvaal Council, which, while acknowledging the authority of the Natal Volksraad, recognized Potgieter as head commandant, with powers which effectively gave him exclusive authority in the Transvaal.

Potchefstroom grew and prospered, but Potgieter remained as obsessed as ever with finding a coastal outlet. It was with this in mind that, in the winter of 1840, he made his first journey to Delagoa Bay. As always, the men were accompanied by their wives, children and servants. They crossed the Highveld plain to the Drakensberg escarpment, through the valley later to become the site of Andries-Ohrigstad. The terrain became increasingly difficult; sometimes it took days to find a suitable path across the mountainous obstacles. At one point they appeared to have reached total impasse, until one of their men, Casper Kruger (father of the fifteen-year old Paul), after scouting for several days, found a way down to the valley. The original track over this pass, named Kaspersnek after the elder Kruger, can still be seen: it leads off from the dirt road between Pilgrim's Rest and Bourke's Luck.

They crossed the valley, dragged their wagons up the steep slope on the other side, finally reached the rounded summit of Graskop to look down over the escarpment, and were then forced to modify their plans: there was a sheer drop of a thousand metres before them. The wives and families were left behind to camp on the Graskop plain while the men went ahead on horseback. It was agreed that, failing their return by an appointed day, the wagons were to make their way back to Potchefstroom. Farewells were said, and the men rode away along a game track leading down by Kowyn's Pass to the Lowveld.

Although the journey took longer than they had anticipated, the men arrived safely at Delagoa Bay. There, Potgieter was welcomed by Governor Antonio Gamitto, who had received Trichardt two years before, and from him Potgieter learned of Trichardt's tragic end.

The two men became firm friends as well as potential partners: Gamitto professed enthusiasm about a commercial arrangement, but was worried about the length and difficulty of the route from Potchefstroom to Delagoa Bay. Perhaps, he suggested, it would be possible to start a town somewhere along the way, from which it would be easier to trade? Much encouraged, Potgieter and his companions set out on their return journey.

By now the women who had stayed behind had given up hope of ever seeing their menfolk emerge from the plain below. Their hearts were heavy, and as an expression of their mood, they named the river beside which they were outspanned the Treur – the 'River of Sorrow'. Finally, as the allotted time ran out, they reluctantly began the return journey.

A few days later, though, as they approached the rim of the valley of the Mdhlazi River, a tributary of the Treur, they heard the drumming of hoofs and the sound of shots and saw their menfolk riding up. There were tears of happiness at the reunion, and they were inspired to give a new name to the Mdhlazi. It became the Blyde River – the 'River of Joy'. The party returned to Potchefstroom with high hopes for a new trade route to the sea.

By now the Voortrekker communities had begun to attract the attention of the outside world. In March 1842 a Dutch trader in Amsterdam, Georg Ohrig, sent out a ship, the *Brazilia*, to deliver his representative, Jean Smellekamp, to Port Natal. But the wheel of fortune for the Natal Trekkers turned once more. The small local colony of English settlers and traders, allies against the Zulus not so long before, now laid claim to the whole region. When Smellekamp returned for a second visit in May 1843, he was refused permission to land at Port Natal. In the circumstances, the agent had little choice but to go on to Delagoa Bay. When Potgieter learned of his arrival, he made a second journey to the bay to meet the Dutchman. At the same time, he finalized a trade pact with the Portuguese government.

From Smellekamp, Potgieter also learned of the latest piece of British legislation. This was the Cape of Good Hope Punishment Bill, in terms of which the Governor of the Cape Colony proclaimed jurisdiction over all territory below latitude 25 degrees south. Such a ruling would prove difficult, if not impossible, to enforce but it nevertheless had a decisive effect on Potgieter's policy in the next few months.

With the promise of trade through Delagoa Bay secured, he returned to Potchefstroom. But the British were progressively taking over Natal, the political situation was approaching the point of crisis and Potgieter's worst fears seemed to have been realized. Consequently, he formally severed links with the disintegrating Natal Republic. In April 1844 he declared the Transvaal an independent state, that of Potchefstroom-Winburg, and formed a puppet Citizens Council. Disillusionment set in among the farmers of Natal; many moved back through the Drakensberg to swell the population of the new state. Then, in February 1845, the British declared Natal a Crown Colony.

Potgieter had ruled off the 25 degree mark on the map, and found that part of the territory north of the Vaal, including Potchefstroom itself, lay to the south of the line. The only answer was yet again to trek, north, beyond the offending demarcation. He would establish a new capital for his infant Republic, one which would be within reach of the port at Delagoa Bay.

On 7 May, 1845 a party of 36 men, led by their fiery and indomitable patriarch, set forth from 'Chief Potgieter's Stream' on the long road to the north-east. Six weeks later, shivering in the bitter cold, they came to the high valleys of the eastern Transvaal escarpment. They made their way down into a well-watered area, some thirty kilometres north of the 25 degree mark. On 5 July Potgieter met the Pedi chief Sekwati, he who had drunk beer seven years before with Louis Trichardt. Now the amiable old man granted Potgieter the right to settle in the valley he had chosen. A village plan was quickly and enthusiastically drawn up, complete with water-furrows and space for a fort. In accordance with the Voortrekker custom of choosing place names from a combination of sources, it was named Andries-Ohrigstad, after Potgieter and the Dutch merchant, Ohrig. They had come to the end of their journey, and, they hoped, to the beginning of a new and settled life.

Putting down roots

At first, everything went well. The climate in the winter months of first arrival was clear and cool. The land was fertile, and the farmsteads were soon built and crops planted. Nearby valleys were thronged with game, and there was never a lack of ready meat. Water was abundant in the bowl of hills. Potgieter's every hope seemed to have been realized.

A collection of modest mud-brick and thatch buildings appeared; wagons continued to roll in from the west, and by the end of July 1845 there were a thousand souls living in and around Andries-Ohrigstad. The village clustered around its fort, with its sturdy outer defence wall. A rudimentary building served as the Volksraad. Other basic structures of a settled society included a prison, and the foundations of a church, though this was never to be completed. By the end of the first year there were about forty dwellings. In time, too, a number of trading stores opened for business, run by enterprising Portuguese merchants from the east.

Over all this loomed the brooding, patriarchal personality of Potgieter. He was Head Commandant, and also a member of the nine-man Volksraad, convened for the first time on 1 August, 1845. In theory, at least, this was supposed to be a republican body, voicing the needs and opinions of the people. In reality it existed simply to rubber-stamp Potgieter's decisions.

Where the council members were of Potgieter's own opinion, the system worked well enough. But a party within the body of the Volksraad soon appeared, one with a mind of its own, a group largely comprising refugees from Natal. There, the Volksraad indeed had been a democratic institution, respected by leaders and people alike. Among those who had served on it was Jacobus Burger, popularly known as 'Lawaai'. Burger had acted as Secretary of the Natal parliamentary body, and he now became the Secretary of the Volksraad in Andries-Ohrigstad.

Inevitably Burger and Potgieter failed to see eye to eye. Potgieter had led the trek, founded the town; now he intended to rule it after his own fashion. But Burger and his supporters were not to be intimidated, even by such an experienced browbeater as the Head Commandant. They clashed over a wide range of issues, from the treatment of the local Africans to the granting of licences to traders. One of the latter provided the catalyst of particularly bitter strife. His name was Henry Hartley – an Englishman and therefore something of a rarity in a society ordered by Potgieter's generally Anglophobic edicts. Hartley arrived in the flourishing little village hoping for a chance to trade with the Trekkers. Potgieter encouraged his application, but the 'Natal party' led by Burger, perhaps remembering their treatment at the hands of Hartley's countrymen in their former land, were adamantly opposed to the award of a licence. Thus were sown the seeds of a mighty discord, one which provided the backcloth for all the other troubles soon to beset Andries-Ohrigstad.

One of the first setbacks involved the principal purpose of founding the village: trade. Most of the farmers were indifferent to commercial opportunity. Once they were settled on their land they tended to forget that the outside world existed. They looked after their crops and their expanding herds. Hunting expeditions provided both pleasure and profit, particularly in the first seasons before the farms began to produce good yields. There were elephant and hippo in the area; ivory was one of the few acceptable cash items. The main problem, however, stemmed from the nature of the Lowveld itself. None of the hazards and inhibitions of the region had diminished since Trichardt and his trek had limped through it.

The settlement made its first serious attempt to find a route from Andries-Ohrigstad to the coast in October 1845. Potgieter organized a party of 26 men under young Carolus Trichardt, son of the former Trekker leader. On the face of it, he was ideal for the job: he knew the Bushveld, and he had a working acquaintance-ship with Portuguese. Unfortunately, though, he was as stubborn as his father had been diplomatic, sullen and boastful by turns.

The party set out on their search for a path to Delagoa Bay, 250 kilometres to the south-east. They managed to cross the Lowveld without incident but then, about ten kilometres from the port, saw fit to stop and put up a series of boundary markers – a tactless move, to say the least. In effect, by doing so they were claiming most of the Bushveld for the Trekkers, who had been six months in the area, leaving the Portuguese, whose settlement was already 300 years old, with a narrow coastal strip. This done, they blithely went on to confer with the Governor before returning home. The reaction was predictable: hard on their heels came a Pedi messenger bearing a letter from the Governor to Potgieter. The offending beacons had been found, and His Excellency would be pleased if the Head Commandant would refrain from sending anyone else to the coast. In a towering rage, Potgieter rounded on the party, vented his formidable fury on them and sent Carolus, cap in hand, back to Delagoa Bay to make formal apology.

Boer-Portuguese relations were thus hastily patched up, but other difficulties, already encountered by Trichardt, would not be so easily soluble: the way to the coast was uncertain at best, and heavily infested with malaria and 'fly'. Coupled with the indifference of most of the farmers to trade, this effectively precluded direct traffic. From then on, trade was conducted largely through a handful of Portuguese merchants.

Among them was the remarkable João Albasini, who had arrived at Delagoa Bay from Portugal in 1831, at the age of eighteen, since when he had become renowned for his hunting and trading exploits, acquiring the name 'Juwawa' from the local tribesmen. He had met both Louis Trichardt and Potgieter on their visits to Delagoa Bay. Now, seeing a chance for profit, he quickly organized a route of his own, one which in due course was to become the famed Old Wagon Trail of the transport-riders. He built a shack on the banks of the Sabie River at the edge of the fever country, at a spot later to be called Pretorius Kop. Here, for several years, he lived a solitary life, running his caravan trade to the interior, enlivening the monotony with spells of elephant hunting. Then, early in 1847, he married a Trekker girl, Gertina Janse van Rensburg, niece of the lost Johannes van Rensburg, and with her he moved to Andries-Ohrigstad, where he struck a bargain with the villagers: in return for information about his tsetse-free route, he would have free title to an erf in the village. If the trail turned out to be not quite as fly-free as he had promised, it did at least offer a usable track which, by the end of the decade, had become well established.

By now, though, the internal rifts in the delicate social fabric of Andries-Ohrigstad had begun to open dangerously wide. Conflict between aging patriarch and rebellious Volksraad intensified with the arrival of more Trekkers from Natal. Not only did they swell the population, but they added to the ranks of the Natal party, giving them the upper hand over Potgieter's supporters.

With this kind of leverage Burger was able to introduce a new Constitution, one based on that of the defunct Natal Republic. While Potgieter could retain the rank of Head Commandant, he would be constitutionally subordinate to the Volksraad's authority. In retaliation, Potgieter claimed to rule by virtue of his treaty with Sekwati, a tactic which neither convinced nor intimidated his opposition. Indeed, Burger replied with a treaty of his own – with Mswati, king of the Swazis and a territorial rival of Sekwati. Signed on 25 July, 1846, it granted the Republic all the land between the Crocodile and Olifants rivers.

The controversy escalated. Potgieter, seeing his power eroded, reacted wildly, accusing Burger of a host of crimes. He had the Secretary arrested, and in September abolished the Volksraad altogether.

By now the entire community was divided, physically as well as politically, the Potgieter party confining itself to the north side of the village, the Natal party dug in on the south side. The settlers were even divided in death – each group maintained its own cemetery!

After the assault on Burger, the Natal men quickly rallied and rescued their leader. Trigger-fingers were itching; civil war a real threat. But at the eleventh hour the crisis was averted. In March 1847 a mass meeting was held and, after long deliberation, the more sensible spirits persuaded their leaders to agree to arbitration by Jean Smellekamp, Ohrig's roving agent, when next he came to Delagoa Bay.

The year 1847 continued to be a busy one for the embattled Hendrik Potgieter. Troubles within were now compounded by assaults from without.

In the early days of settlement, relations with Sekwati's tribesmen had been amicable enough. Sekwati himself was a peace-loving man, and had treated visitors to and settlers in his realm with courtesy and hospitality. But cattle were, by long tradition, legitimate plunder and soon after the first farms were settled, stock thefts and night raids began. These led to retaliatory forays by the farmers, which in turn provoked larger-scale attacks on the village itself, so that protective walls had to be built around strategic points. Despite this, the assaults continued, impelling Potgieter to launch a punitive raid on the Pedi in 1847, and in the same year to organize a large expedition. With over 200 men he rode north across the Limpopo into the lands recently secured by his old enemy, Mzilikazi. From there, after some inconclusive skirmishing, the settlers returned home to a village that was already well on its way towards total disintegration.

Many of Potgieter's own followers, weary of endless discord, had quietly loaded up their wagons and returned to Potchefstroom. More important, the community was collapsing in the face of a natural threat infinitely more dangerous than human intransigence: the fever of the Lowveld, which was finding its devastating way into the mountains.

The village had been laid out in the cool and deceptive months of winter. But in summer the valley became a heat-trap, the sun beating down with merciless ferocity. Under these conditions, the sickness spread quickly. Hunters and traders returning from the Lowveld brought the plague with them. Each summer the outbreaks became worse, and many died. Others, galvanized by fear, returned to the healthier territory to the west.

By the beginning of 1848 Andries-Ohrigstad was almost a ghost town. Among those to go were Hendrik Potgieter and his followers. In a mass exodus some six hundred-strong, they trekked away northwards to the Soutpansberg, where Potgieter founded his third and last settlement. The habit of argument, long ingrained, went with them. Again they wrangled among themselves, and the name of the Strydpoort, the 'Pass of Strife', aptly reflects the nature of these restless, independent and quarrelsome people.

Left behind were the men of the Natal party and the Volksraad presided over by 'Lawaai' Burger, relieved of the burden of Potgieter's disruptive presence. But their new-found peace of mind proved to be short-lived: the summer of 1848-49 brought the heaviest outbreak of fever yet, killing scores of people, including Burger himself. Indeed the death-rate was so high that the survivors were unable to cope with the disposal of the dead. Corpses lay in the blistering heat for days before removal, and often three, four and more were hastily buried in a single grave.

It became clear that wherever the capital of the eastern Transvaal was formally proclaimed, it would not be at Ohrigstad. The town was doomed. The survivors made plans to move elsewhere, to higher ground farther to the south, out of the malaria belt. So, in September 1849, yet another trek began.

The first site was chosen about 45 kilometres from Ohrigstad, on the farms Boschhoek, Waterval and Enkeldoorn, but it transpired that the area was short of water, and the settlers moved on to the farm Rietspruit, belonging to one Johannes Coetser and well watered by the nearby Sterkspruit and Spekboom rivers. To the local Pedi the area was known as Masising, or 'Place of the Long Grass'. But the Trekkers, their hardships still vivid in memory, called their new village Lydenburg, the 'Town of Suffering'.

Despite its gloom-laden name, the village was to survive, grow and thrive, though not without the usual quota of bickering among the town worthies.

It was laid out on a simple grid-plan. Four streets ran in a north-south direction, while another four intersected with them from east to west. A square was paced out on Kantoor Street, between Kerk and Mark Streets, and here were built the Landdrost's office and the town gaol and, in 1851, a start was made on the construction of an imposing new NG Kerk, the only one in the Transvaal to remain within the Cape Synod. In 1852, when the church had reached roof height, the admirable Dr Andrew Murray arrived to conduct its first service. Within a year the building was complete, its yellowwood beams the only surviving memento of the church in Andries-Ohrigstad. And as at Ohrigstad, defence walls were erected around parts of the town, including the Landdrost's office and the church.

Thus were justice and the spiritual needs of the small community served. So, too, was education. Until now, most of the Voortrekker children had gained what little schooling they could claim on the hoof, picking their way through their Biblical texts to the creak of an ox-wagon. Now they could delight in a simple rectangular schoolhouse with four shuttered windows and a thatched roof, little different in style from the average farmstead. Here they were supervised by Willem Poen, a Hollander specially brought in to teach the local youngsters Bible and catechism and the secular subjects. He started work in December 1852 on an annual salary of £15, which meagre amount was drawn from church funds. Later, the church asked the Volksraad for assistance in meeting the salary bill, then gradually phased out its own contribution. This may have been due to friction between the teacher and the first predikant of the church, Ds Van Heyningen, with whom Poen was constantly at loggerheads, so much so that he eventually abandoned teaching altogether to become the town postmaster and auctioneer.

Free of fever, Lydenburg made healthy progress, and in doing so it developed ambitions of its own. The spirit of independence was reflected in disputes with other centres, from Potchefstroom to Soutpansberg, on any and every imaginable subject – and in the town's finest hour, the Lydenburg declaration of independence. This startling move was triggered by developments elsewhere. During the months of Ohrigstad's and Lydenburg's conception and birth, great events had taken place farther south.

After the British occupation of Natal, Andries Pretorius, champion of Voortrekker settlement in that green and pleasant land, had retreated to the Transvaal. There, he continued to nurture

Lydenburg's first school-house. Until it was built in 1852, the children had received their tuition on trek, learning their Biblical texts to the accompaniment of creaking wagon wheels. Other buildings erected at around the same time were the Landdrost's office and the gaol, each of which faced onto the small town square, and the impressive NG Kerk building. The renowned Dr Andrew Murray conducted the church's first service.

visions of Trekker unity, of a consolidated Boer nation under his own leadership. In June 1848 he rode south of the Vaal to lay claim to the Orange Free State, now under British sovereignty, only to be roundly defeated at the Battle of Boomplaats on 29 August. He fled back across the river carrying a price of £2 000 on his head. Still defiant, he retaliated by offering 2 000 head of cattle in return for the Governor of the Cape Colony, dead or alive, but the gesture did little to ease his situation. His fortunes had reached their lowest ebb.

But the Transvaal was nothing if not a place of sudden reversals. As at Andries-Ohrigstad and Lydenburg, there were many refugees from Natal among the people of Potchefstroom. Ever since Potgieter had abandoned the place three years before with hardly a backward glance, it had been without a leader. Into this position Pretorius now stepped.

Moreover, in a sudden and dramatic change of policy, the British revoked their claim to all the territory below the 'British Line' (the latitude 25 degrees south). Officially, until this moment, the Trekkers north of the line had been outlaws. Now, in January 1852, Pretorius found himself summoned to the Sand River Conference. There the British announced their intention of establishing friendly relations with the Transvaal Republic, and of giving the burghers their charter of freedom. This was duly signed on 17 January. From being an outlaw with a price on his head, Pretorius found himself, with one stroke of a British pen, grandly vindicated. He returned to Potchefstroom a hero.

Thus the man who had once refused to join the Transvaal now became its leader. And Hendrik Potgieter, his long-time rival, was left high and dry on the slopes of the Soutpansberg. Admittedly he was happy enough there. Indeed, he may have felt that he had at last achieved his earthly paradise. After the débâcle at Ohrigstad, he had not repeated the mistake of allowing any democratically elected Volksraad to argue with him. He ruled in lonely splendour, an autocratic chieftain, the 'Great Elephant of the Voortrekkers' as the tribesmen called him. In the Soutpansberg he had established good working relationships with the local chiefs, and had even managed to open up a difficult but usable route through their territory to the sea at Inhambane. To crown these significant successes, Mzilikazi, grown wiser and perhaps more amiable, had sent ambassadors to sue for peace.

In a sense, Potgieter and Pretorius were now morally on equal terms. Each had won victories over great odds, and lost others facing even greater odds. Now, after years of antagonism and mutual mistrust, they were persuaded to come together and to make their peace. On 16 March, 1852 they met at the new town of Rustenburg in the western Transvaal and, after a long private parley in their tent, they emerged before their collected followers with their hands solemnly placed upon the same Bible.

The two men had agreed to share control of the country. Both remained head commandant, with equal powers. But they made another decision at Rustenburg which was to have long-term repercussions and to lead to years of strife. With no legal power to do so, they ordained that, upon their deaths, their sons, Marthinus Wessel Pretorius and Pieter Potgieter, should jointly inherit the mantle of power.

This was almost the last significant move made by either of the two men. Time was running out for the old warriors.

Hendrik Potgieter was approaching sixty and already ailing. In the long years of wandering he had buried four wives, and was now married to his fifth. After returning to his lair in the Soutpansberg, he led some 320 men on a last sortie, in August 1852, in retaliation against the cattle raids of Sekwati's people. They reached into the heart of the chief's mountain stronghold, called Phiring, or 'Place of Hyenas', besieging it for several weeks and cutting off the Pedi from their water supply. Towards the end the tribesmen were reduced to drinking the foul liquid from the stomachs of their slaughtered animals, and managed to avoid total annihilation only through the initiative of Sekwati's son, Sekhukhune, who succeeded in breaking out of the Trekkers' lines and bringing water back to the survivors. A few days later the siege was lifted, and the commando returned to the Soutpansberg, driving before it 5 000 head of Pedi cattle.

By now, Hendrik Potgieter was a dying man. He retired to his farm to spend his last days on his verandah, surrounded by his many children and relatives. One of his last acts was to conclude a treaty of peace with his old enemy, Mzilikazi. He died on 16 December, 1852: a peaceful end to a lifetime filled with bitter dispute, brutal war and heroic exploration. He was followed seven months later by Andries Pretorius, who died at fifty-four.

It was now that the latent unwisdom of the last pact between the two leaders became patently clear. Their sons took control, Marthinus Pretorius at Potchefstroom and Pieter Potgieter in the Soutpansberg. Tragically, the young Potgieter was soon killed in a campaign against the Makapan. By the law of succession, he was succeeded by his nine-year-old son, Andries. Until the boy should come of age, power was placed in the hands of a regent – Stephanus Schoeman, who had married Pieter Potgieter's widow. When the boy died soon afterwards, Schoeman, without legal right to do so, took over as Commandant-General. Had Schoeman been a wise ruler, all might have turned out well enough, but he was a difficult, truculent individual with scant regard for popular

Vignettes of Lydenburg. *Clockwise from right:* three of the mysterious Iron Age masks found at the 'Head Site' outside the town and now displayed in its museum; Lydenburg's well-patronized Standard Hotel, pictured around the turn of the century; the offices of the local newspaper; the old Loreto Convent.
Below: 1 500-year-old pottery exhibits – precious archaeological finds from one of the some fifty mountain cave sites in the region – in Lydenburg's museum.

opinion. For the time being, however, Marthinus Pretorius chose to ignore the usurper, and turned his attention elsewhere.

Though he appears to have inherited his father's passion for Voortrekker unity, the young Pretorius lacked Andries's political acumen. After orchestrating his own election as the new Commandant-General, he convened a conference in Potchefstroom, which appointed a commission to design a constitution for the Republic, which Pretorius now renamed the South African Republic. Predictably, he was elected first President of the new State.

Unhappily, in the course of this process, he had made a number of tactical errors. His election took place not by public vote, but by a special sitting of the Volksraad. This highly unconstitutional proceeding created bitter resentment in the other towns. Schoeman, offered a post in the government, angrily turned it down: he had no intention of serving under Pretorius, or anyone else for that matter. And the people of Lydenburg, very conscious of their growing municipal status, took offence at not having been consulted. In particular they felt that their town, not Potchefstroom, should have been the scene of the conference. Their reaction was swift and uncompromising: they decided to secede and form a republic of their own.

On 11 March, 1857, with all due ceremony, the Lydenburgers ran up the newly designed flag of 'De Republiek Lydenburg en Zuid-Afrika'. And having declared themselves independent, they went on to claim generous boundaries: the Republic, they insisted, comprised all the land from the Olifants River in the north to Zululand in the south, and from a line along the Elands River in the west to the edge of the Bushveld in the east. Sekwati and his tribe were granted the area between the Olifants and the Steelpoort rivers.

As with the troublesome events in the Soutpansberg, Pretorius at first ignored all this, for he had set his mind to other plans. Among these, one had already borne fruit. In February 1857 he had started a new settlement north of Potchefstroom, that of Pretoria. It was situated on the banks of the Apies River, once the scene of Mzilikazi's camp. In fact it went through several changes of name, including Pretoriusdorp and Pretorium, before settling down as Pretoria.

With his family name thus immortalized, Pretorius continued with a career marked more by failure than success. He did, however, manage to persuade Lydenburg, after three years of independence, to rejoin the South African Republic. As a condition for their return to the fold, the Lydenburgers held out for a change of capital, insisting that this should now be Pretoria. The agreement was formally ratified, after a year of complicated negotiations, on 3 April, 1860.

Pretorius's attempt to weld the Republic and the Orange Free State into a single nation, however, met with less success. As a compromise he suggested the extraordinary and quite unconstitutional expedient of acting as a kind of roving President. He took six months leave of absence to govern the Free State, then returned across the Vaal to Pretoria to take up the Transvaal's reigns again. By now, though, the Transvaal Volksraad had lost patience. They told Pretorius outright to choose one country or the other. Deeply offended, he abandoned his claim to the Transvaal and returned to the Free State. But Potchefstroom, dominated by his supporters, now complicated matters by refusing to accept the Volksraad's ruling. They unilaterally reversed its decision and re-elected Pretorius as leader and, because he was still absent, they appointed Stephanus Schoeman as Acting President.

It was an ill-advised move.

As soon as he was installed, the new ruler convened a meeting of the Volksraad and then ordered the arrest of the very men who had, quite illegally, appointed him in the first place. This act of treachery enraged Pretorius's supporters. With the young Field Cornet Paul Kruger at their head, they marched on Pretoria to deal with Schoeman. Before they reached the capital, however, Pretorius arrived back. He immediately convened a new Volksraad drawn from among his own supporters. They sacked Schoeman on the spot, along with his retinue of officials.

Confusion now degenerated into chaos; political dissension into a sporadic, curious, almost comic-opera kind of civil war. Despite his formal rejection, Schoeman refused to relinquish authority and Kruger and his men saddled up once again to march to Pretoria. Schoeman fled the town, and for the next two years he and Kruger played a game of military cat-and-mouse up and down the plains of the Transvaal. There were plenty of alarums and excursions, but casualties were few. The main consequence of the conflict was to inhibit any semblance of settled government, and to bring the Republic to the brink of bankruptcy. And cattle-thieves had a field-day.

By now it had become clear that young Marthinus Pretorius was disastrously incompetent. He survived another election in 1869, but only by a narrow margin. Finally, in 1871, after bungling negotiations with the Cape over the diamond fields at Kimberley, he was turned out of office by an irate Volksraad. He disappeared from political life, and with him went the principle of hereditary rule within the Trekker community.

The people of the Transvaal now made a momentous decision: to look for a President beyond their own borders. The elders consulted with the steadfast and able President Brand of the Orange Free State, who recommended Thomas François Burgers, a Dutch Reformed predikant who ministered at Hanover in the Cape Colony. Up to this point Burgers, though intelligent and well-educated, had little experience of public life beyond the narrow confines of his parish. His only entry into the limelight, and a modest enough one, had been a disagreement on theological principle with his conservative superiors in the church a few years before. He had courageously and successfully taken his case to the higher authority of the Supreme Court.

At the time of the offer from the Transvaal Volksraad Burgers was 37 years old, and married to a Scotswoman named Mary Bryson. He accepted the challenge, and was inaugurated at Pretoria with much pomp on 27 June, 1872. After the cheers had died down, though, he took a closer look at the job he had so gallantly accepted.

Burgers was not encouraged by what he saw.

The affairs of the South African Republic were in an appalling state of confusion. The currency was almost worthless paper money: the Republican Pound, the despised 'blueback', which one was happy enough to pay out, less happy to receive. Most transactions were carried out on the basis of promissory notes. The paucity of hard cash in the marketplace had long encouraged venality and petty corruption, particularly among the ill-paid officials.

Burgers, a conscientious and upright man, tackled the root of the problem. He began with a wholesale sacking of officials; insisted on accurate and comprehensive bookkeeping in all government departments (one previous official had kept all his records 'in his head'). He also managed to persuade the Cape Commercial Bank to lend the tottering Republic £60 000. Despite all his efforts, however, the country remained precariously balanced on the brink of insolvency, its very survival at stake.

But then, unexpectedly, there came hope, and eventually rescue. The news drifted in quietly, carried across the great grassland plains of the Transvaal like a whisper on the wind. Its principle message was contained in a single, magical word: gold. For within a day's ride of Lydenburg, among the valleys and streams of the Drakensberg escarpment, had been found the first traces of the yellow metal which was to change the face of the land, and to alter forever the course of its history.

The pilgrim arrives

The existence of gold in Africa had long been known. Early Dutch settlers at the Cape were intrigued by reports of the legendary land of Monomotapa, supposedly situated at the very heart of the 'Dark Continent' and believed to be fabulously endowed with the yellow metal. Inspired by these tales, Jan van Riebeeck had gone so far as to send an expedition, in 1658, in search of this alluring land. It had come to a halt, however, on the banks of the Great Berg River – the first but far from the last treasure hunt to end in empty-handed despondency.

In 1806 the traveller John Barrow published a map of a surmised goldfield in the interior. It showed a high mountain range to the north of the Vaal River where he confidently, if vaguely, predicted that gold would be found. Barrow's map might have been somewhat elaborate and imaginative, but fragments of real evidence were beginning to emerge. The first Trekkers in the Transvaal noted with interest that many of the local black women wore gold ornaments, and hunters and traders brought back from the north reports of mysterious ancient mine-workings deep in the bush, long abandoned.

It was only in the mid-nineteenth century, however, that a systematic search was undertaken, by the English geologist John Henry Davis. He had met the Trekker leader Andries Pretorius at the Sand River Convention in 1852, and Pretorius had invited him to look for gold in the Transvaal. Davis, accompanied by his ten-year-old son, spent a year prospecting, but though there are conflicting reports, the general concensus is that he found no gold.

The second and more fully documented search took place the following year, by the 25-year-old Pieter Jacob Marais who, notwithstanding his youth, was already an experienced prospector. He had been one of the 'forty-niners', joining the great gold-rush to California in 1849 and had then worked the Bendigo Field in Australia. In neither of these places had he made his fortune so, remembering the legends and the rumours, he returned to try his luck in the country of his birth.

Marais arrived in Potchefstroom in September 1853, and from there he made his way north to the Crocodile River, an upper branch of the Limpopo. Energetic panning in the river gravel soon brought him a modicum of luck. In his diary for 7 October he noted that he had 'Found a few specks of gold in the River Crocodile'. The following day, at the nearby Jukskei River, he recorded: 'Found more gold.'

At the end of November he returned to Potchefstroom, convinced that payable quantities were at hand, and that it simply needed a determined search to find them. On 1 December, he approached that august body, the Transvaal Volksraad, and showed them his finds. In all truth these were modest enough, but he was nevertheless sufficiently bold to predict that there was more gold in the Transvaal than in California and Australia put together!

Marais was, of course, wrong. There was more gold in the Transvaal than in the rest of the world put together. Almost beneath their feet there lay vast seams of it. Indeed, the grains in the Crocodile and Jukskei rivers had originally been washed down from the Witwatersrand deposits. Carried away by the prospector's eloquence, the Volksraad were sufficiently moved to offer Marais practical encouragement. He was promised a reward of £5 000 in the event of his finding payable gold, a share in future proceeds, and the post of mine manager. To their generosity in giving away what had not yet been found, the Volksraad added a somewhat bloodthirsty proviso, a clause in the agreement which stated that:

'Should it happen that P. J. Marais divulges any information about the conditions of the discovered gold mines, or anything in connection therewith to any foreign power, government or particular person, and by doing so causes the independence of the Republic to be disturbed or threatened in any way, such action shall be punished with the penalty of death and no extenuating circumstances will be taken into consideration.' Despite this threat, news of Marais' quest soon spread.

Nevertheless, with his warning in his pocket, he eagerly set off for the north, and during the next two years energetically scoured almost every part of the Transvaal. He concentrated his efforts on the river courses, panning for alluvial gold of the kind found predominantly in California and Australia. Many a time he found a faint 'tail' in his iron pan, but nothing payable. Finally, weary and dejected, he returned to Potchefstroom to report failure. The Volksraad shared his disappointment, though this was mixed with vague suspicion. After all the boasts, the golden predictions so confidently expressed, could Marais really have found nothing? Or was he hiding something from them? They determined to question the young prospector a little more closely, and accordingly invited him to present himself before them. But Marais, perhaps remembering that ferocious penalty clause, took fright. At the end of August 1855 he quietly decamped from the Transvaal to the Cape, where he settled down to the less exciting but more lucrative life of a Dordrecht storekeeper.

Marais' experience had demonstrated all too clearly what was to become a central fact of life for many men in the years to come – that there was all the difference in the world between traces of gold in a pan and payable deposits. Perhaps the best example of the contrast between dream and reality was in the career of Karl Gottlieb Mauch.

Born in Stettin in Germany in 1837, Mauch had, as a young man, developed a passionate interest in geology and botany, and an ambition to travel and to explore Africa, whose fascination he had sensed in the museums and zoos of Europe. Lack of money held him back, but finally he managed to scrape enough together for a passage to Africa, arriving in Durban Bay in January 1865. From there he travelled the short distance to Pietermaritzburg, where he stayed long enough to familiarize himself with Dutch and English. Then he pushed on, eagerly, towards the land of his dreams, hitching a lift on a transport wagon, first to Rustenburg, and then on to Potchefstroom.

Mauch was an extravagant personality, and his personal motto a bold one. 'Go anywhere, do anything!' he proclaimed, and soon showed he was prepared to live up to it fully. After exploring and prospecting for minerals around Potchefstroom, he headed north on a hunting trip to the Limpopo. On his return he met the trader and hunter Henry Hartley, he whose desire for a trading licence had caused such friction in Andries-Ohrigstad a few years earlier. Hartley was also a large character, and had many tales to tell of his adventures. Like many other hunters, in the course of his wandering he had come across the abandoned remains of old mine workings, which he believed were the site of the Biblical Ophir. These accounts soon fired Mauch's always inflammable imagination, and it was not long before he and Hartley agreed to try their luck together.

They set out on an expedition which lasted from May 1866 to January 1867, during which time they crossed Kipling's 'great grey-green greasy Limpopo' into the wilds of Matabeleland. Mauch gathered over a hundred different mineral specimens, with which they returned to Potchefstroom. There he displayed his finds at the country's first agricultural show. (The Transvaal Agricultural Society had been formed the previous year, with Marthinus Pretorius as its first President.) The show was opened with all due ceremony on 20 March, 1867 with a grand display which included farm produce, collections of wild animals, tame ostriches, karosses, and tribal ornaments and weapons. There was also a prize for the best mineral display. Mauch carried off the £5 award with his exhibit, which had attracted a lot of speculative interest.

Later in the same year, the two explorers again set off. They fossicked along the Limpopo, and went north to inspect the Zimbabwe Ruins. Then, while exploring along the Tati River, Mauch discovered traces of gold. They returned post-haste to Potchefstroom in a fever of excitement. There Mauch reported his find in glowing terms to a local newspaper, the *Transvaal Argus*, dwelling at length on the size and wealth of the distant goldfields. Great fortunes, he declared, had once been made there, and would soon be made again. The newspaper added a few romantic touches of its own and the story was printed on 4 December as Mauch's dramatic rediscovery of 'King Solomon's Mines'.

The report caused an instant sensation, within and far beyond the Transvaal's borders – for the story was reprinted around the world. Overnight, it awoke the gold-lust of thousands. Even while Mauch was elaborating his oracular vision, men began to arrive – from the Cape across the Vaal River, from Durban, and across the Lowveld from Lourenço Marques, all bent on reaching the Tati, a river only a handful had hitherto even heard of.

The prospectors who converged on Potchefstroom alerted the Transvaal government, which was determined to stay one jump ahead of the newcomers. Early in February 1868 the Volksraad sent Commandant Jan Viljoen to visit Mzilikazi and the Mangwato chief, Matsheng, who governed in the area around the Tati River. Viljoen made agreements with the two rulers and, at the same time, attempted to gain control over a larger area. President Pretorius issued a grandiose proclamation claiming all land where gold might be discovered – a somewhat ambitious statement since the Transvaal was on the point of financial collapse and in no position to control new territory.

Close on Viljoen's heels came the first men of the rush, using Potchefstroom as their base and the starting-point of their journey to the Tati region. Among those who set out from the town was a certain Captain George Black, who led a party of nine men and was accompanied by the ubiquitous Henry Hartley, who had agreed to act as guide in return for a cut of the profits. They set out on 11 March, with their belongings loaded onto a wagon adorned with the British and Transvaal flags and bearing the brave legend *Nil Desperandum*. They arrived at the Tati River, which they christened the New Victoria Gold Field, and fell with a will to prospecting and digging.

Alas, they had no more luck than had Marais or Mauch. After seven weeks of back-breaking labour in a ten-metre shaft, Black and his party had recovered no more than half an ounce of gold. Bitterly frustrated, they gave up the effort and returned to Potchefstroom against the still-oncoming tide of hopeful prospectors. Among these were some wonderful characters, including the eccentric Sir John Swinburne, a relative of the poet Algernon Charles Swinburne. Sir John arrived in Potchefstroom in February 1869 with three baggage wagons and a portable 12-horse-power engine, mounted on wheels and drawn by oxen. The townspeople turned out in force to witness the strange cavalcade, and were particularly impressed by the engine, the first of its kind in the Transvaal. Swinburne soon made his mark on the town, paying £1 250 in cash for a large building in which to house the headquarters of his grandly-named London & Limpopo Mining Company, one of a number of local enterprises set up with financial backing from London. He also proposed to the Transvaal

government that he take over the blueback paper currency at ten shillings in the pound, as well as every unsold farm. The London & Limpopo would then run the Republic much in the fashion of a chartered company. Financially straitened as they were, though, the Volksraad declined to mortgage themselves to this persuasive British aristocrat.

Despite his fund of both money and confidence, Swinburne and his engine met with as little success as all the other expeditions to the Tati River, finding only small, tantalizing traces of gold. One by one the ventures foundered, leaving behind a floating detritus of prospectors who had had enough money to get to Africa, but not enough to get out again. The real beneficiaries of the Tati River episode were the storekeepers and traders of Potchefstroom who, while the rush lasted, enjoyed something approaching boom conditions, selling everything from picks and shovels to food, liquor and transport to the northward-bound hopefuls. The Transvaal Conveyance Company, for example, conducted a highly profitable business carrying passengers and their belongings to the goldfield at a rate of £10 a head.

The Pied Piper of all this, Karl Gottlieb Mauch, seemed undeterred by the lack of results. In April 1868 he entered another mineral exhibit at the second show held in Potchefstroom, and again carried off the £5 prize. His financial situation had begun to deteriorate, but funds arrived from Germany and he was soon on the road again. With two companions he set out on his third venture, which this time took him to the east – to the Lydenburg area. He worked his way along the Drakensberg escarpment, enjoying the splendour of the scenery and, as always, daily expected to make the big strike. He never did make it, but if he brought nothing away from the eastern Transvaal, he did leave something of himself behind for posterity: his name on the Mauchberg. He wandered back to the Limpopo, where he spent several months. After an interlude in pursuit of diamonds in the Bloemhof area, he returned to his first love – prospecting in the Soutpansberg. Other expeditions took him to Lourenço Marques, down the Vaal River in search of diamonds, and along the Zambezi River to the sea.

Finally, Mauch gave up the quest. Poverty-stricken, he managed to find a free berth on a French ship returning to Marseilles, and spent the rest of his life in Germany, dreaming of Africa and its elusive wealth. Rich though he was in memory of adventure, his cash return had been almost negligible: from all his years in the veld his sole profit had been the £10 won at the Transvaal Agricultural shows.

Nevertheless, his legacy to the new territories of the interior was considerable: his maps of the land, both topographical and geological, were outstanding contributions to nineteenth century exploration and, in some respects, to development; and it was he who first sketched and reported on the mysterious Zimbabwe Ruins.

The main consequence of Mauch's undoubted genius for publicity had been to lure a large number of diggers to the Transvaal. With the prospecting community swelling by the month, the chances of a real find were greatly increased. And it was not long before this happened. It took place in the eastern Transvaal, in the area which Mauch himself had pinpointed: with his customary confidence he had once waved an arm in the general direction of the Blyde River and had foretold: 'Gold will be found there!'

And it was, by a small group of men who arrived in the Transvaal in 1869, fresh from an abortive gold-rush in Natal. They were led by Edward Button, the son of an 1850 Natal settler. With him were George Parsons, one of the leaders of the Natal rush, and James Sutherland, the most experienced of the trio, who had spent twenty years in the Californian fields.

At this time, expeditions to the Tati River were still being organized. Button and his friends, however, had heard of Mauch's prediction for the Lydenburg region. Moreover the area was considerably nearer and more accessible than Tati. They arrived at Lydenburg, from where they turned north-east towards the 'Berg and were soon joined by another prospector, Tom McLachlan, who knew the area well. They searched the valleys already explored by Mauch without, at first, finding anything beyond a few tiny traces. In the winter of 1869, losing heart, they moved north across the Limpopo to the Vubwe River, where they separated. McLachlan stayed in the area to trade, Parsons set off for the Transvaal, while Button and Sutherland drifted to the east and down to the Lowveld. There they panned in a range of mountains they named after the renowned geologist Sir Roderick Murchison. Again they found many traces of gold, but nothing payable. Thereafter, Button worked his way back to Lydenburg, where he panned without success in the local rivers. By now McLachlan and Parsons, too, had made their way back to the escarpment, setting up camp on the Graskop.

It was on a visit to Lydenburg that Edward Button picked up the clue that was to earn him a place in gold-mining history.

Many of the Transvaal's farmers, overcoming their Calvinistic antipathy to the Devil's metal, had fossicked on their own farms. Among these was Jacobus du Preez, who owned the farm Eersteling in the Marabastad area. He found traces of gold in the stream running through his property, and while on a visit to Lydenburg, met Button, told him of the discovery, and invited him to come and prospect on Eersteling.

Almost immediately Button found what he believed to be payable quantities of gold. In a fever of excitement he named his find the 'Natalia' reef and, on 25 September, 1870, sent samples to the Volksraad in Pretoria for inspection. A commission was hastily formed to investigate the claim, from which it returned with two more ounces of Button's gold.

The news spread like a bushfire through the prospecting fraternity. In a bid to beat the competition, Button journeyed to Pretoria. There he was given the title of Gold Commissioner and granted exclusive rights to the gold on Eersteling. Armed with this concession, and with some good samples, he travelled to England. The London merchants were much impressed by the gold he showed them, and by his tales of a great field to be had for the taking. This was a period when international markets were rapidly expanding, and gold was much in demand, and it did not take Button long to persuade the financiers to bankroll his venture. Soon the Transvaal Gold Mining Company, with a capitalization of £50 000 and Button as its general manager, had been registered. Button sailed back to Africa with a twelve-stamp battery for extracting his ore.

By now a small army of prospectors had gathered around Eersteling. Land values soared and every house and empty farmstead in and around Potgietersrus had been commandeered as a diggers' 'hotel', mostly of the most primitive order. With their tents and sluice-boxes, they spread along the river course. Their crushers were improvised affairs, comprising a large boulder over which a plank was roped, see-saw fashion. The motive power for this was supplied by two local Pedi tribesmen, who sat one at either end of the plank, rocking it back and forth while the miners fed their quartz under it. Once crushed, the rock fragments were panned for gold.

Into this scene Button returned with his battery like an avenging angel. The exclusive rights to Eersteling were his, and he had no intention of sharing its undoubted riches with this greedy rabble, whom he forthwith evicted. Then he settled down to work his claim, an activity which soon brought his dreams down to size. True, the diggings produced a little gold, enough at least to pay for the battery, but of larger deposits there was no sign. He was forced to abandon the mine, leaving only a pile of rusty machinery and a few leaky shacks as a dilapidated memorial to his once-high hopes.

As the founder of the first real gold-mining company, Button earned himself a modest place in the annals of the early Transvaal. He also pointed others in the right direction. The prospectors were getting close. Very close, for early in 1873 the first deposits of payable gold were found.

The honours went to Tom McLachlan, who had gone into partnership with Parsons and another miner, Valentine. Spurred on by an offer of a £500 reward from the Republic for the discovery of a viable lode, they concentrated on the Blyde River area. For long their labours went unrewarded, but then their luck changed. South of Sabie was the farm Hendriksdal, which belonged to one Hendrik Coetzer, and on 6 February, 1873, while prospecting the creek running through the farm, the partners found signs of the metal. Feverishly they worked on and eventually, on the slopes of the nearby Spitskop, in a small creek they named McLachlan's Gully, they panned a two-and-a-half ounce sample of gold. A few days later the Landdrost of Lydenburg, A. F. Jansen, inspected the claim and reported it to the Executive Council in Pretoria. On 14 May, 1873 the Spitskop area was declared a public digging, and the next frantic rush was launched.

The arrival of several hundred prospectors inevitably produced new finds, larger than the first. A little to the north of the Spitskop lay the farm Geelhoutboom, on the river which runs down to what are now the Mac Mac Falls. There the farmer Johannes Muller and his son, Diedricht, had become infected with gold-fever. Tom McLachlan had given them some hints on the art of prospecting, and with beginner's luck they almost immediately extracted a rich yield from the river gravel. Soon the alert McLachlan had moved in, purchasing a part of Geelhoutboom. There, he and his partners built a small stone house, which they used as a base for their operations.

Two distinct communities congregated: by the end of March 1873 there were some 200 diggers along the five kilometres of the river at Geelhoutboom, with about the same number at Spitskop. As the camps grew, the Landdrost set up a diggers' committee, which elected a Gold Commissioner, or Sheriff. He was literally a figure out of the Wild West, an American named Major W. MacDonald, tall and scrawny, with a sunburnt face framed by grey ringlets under a battered slouch hat and a cigar permanently clamped between his teeth. He was given the power to register claims, collect fees, and settle disputes from an office which also served as his prospector's tent.

Something resembling a settled community began to develop, though the yields of gold rarely amounted to more than five pennyweights a day. Besides the tents, there were groups of rough shacks and shelters. A gaol was built, and a diggers' police force formed to administer rough but effective justice. Though the diggings were generally peaceful, there was the occasional malefactor, and he received short shrift. One prospector named Taylor, for example, was caught filching letters from the Post Office. He was given a summary trial, sentenced to 25 lashes, had half his beard cut off, and was finally run out of camp.

The feelings of the Transvaal government towards this sudden flurry of activity within its borders were ambivalent. On the one hand there was the indisputable fact that even a hint of gold was enough to improve, vastly, the Republic's fragile credit-rating in the outside world. At the same time, the Volksraad were nervous of the growing number of foreigners descending on their young, hitherto placid and almost exclusively Boer state. To find out more about this possible threat President Thomas Burgers set out on a trip in August 1873, in order to inspect the diggings for himself.

He arrived at Geelhoutboom, where he was given a warm welcome and, in turn, responded with remarkable tact and sympathy. In common with many of the miners, Burgers had something of the dreamer and romantic in him. He soon concluded that these 'Uitlanders' did not represent a genuine risk to his country's character and its integrity. They lived only for gold; the land itself meant nothing to them unless it contained gold; matters political held even less interest. When he had met all the leading digger personalities, the President was shown into MacDonald's tent-office, where he looked through the licences. He was amused to note that every other name began with 'Mac'. Indeed, the list was almost a roll-call of the Highland clans. 'Why, it's all Mac!' he exclaimed, and promptly announced that henceforth the place would be called 'Mac Mac' (its official name, though, remained the New Caledonia Gold Fields). It was a gesture which reinforced Burgers's popularity among the diggers, a fondness that lingered in memory long after the disappearance of the miners, their tents and shacks.

Burgers confirmed the appointment of that 'staunch republican', Major MacDonald, as Gold Commissioner. He also arranged for the promulgation of provisional gold regulations. Licences were to be granted at five shillings a claim per month; each individual could hold a maximum of four claims; a number of minor points concerning the jumping of claims were clarified. Over and above this the miners were asked to draw up a more detailed and comprehensive gold law for themselves. The President listened patiently and sympathetically to complaints, the main difficulties arising from isolation and a dearth of transport. Burgers granted £1 500 for the improvement of the primitive wagon-track to Lydenburg, a job which was in fact completed over the next few months by the diggers themselves.

With government approval and a set of provisional laws both protecting and controlling them, the miners got on with their real work: digging, crushing and panning for fortunes. At Spitskop the yield remained limited and the ground, moreover, was difficult to work. There was little running water, so the miners had to build long races to bring it to the workings from distant steams.

At the height of the Spitskop boom there were probably no more than 200 men in the area. McLachlan's Gully remained the focus of most of the activity, and around it were built the stores and canteens which supplied the diggers. In one creek a German immigrant named Bossman ran a canteen called Squareface, named after a local make of gin. At another spot the Englishman Byerley ran a hotel until a summer rainstorm scoured it clean away. Perhaps the most renowned emporium at Spitskop, though, belonged to a character called Harry Russell. Built of mud and packing-cases supporting a tarpaulin roof, it was both general store and drinking den. Inside, all was chaos, with goods heaped up at random. Russell slept under the counter, and ate off a packing-case lid in a tiny space among his wares. At night the diggers congregated to drink brandy and whisky and to play monte and euchre, generally for low stakes since most of them were impoverished. Sitting in the flickering light of the lantern, dressed in their coarse moleskin trousers, thick woollen jerseys and stout leather boots, they presented a motley crew, held together by a single obsessive topic of conversation. Among them were many who were to achieve immortality of one kind or another in the goldfields in the years to come, men such as Bob Buck, Spanish Joe, Black Sam, Wally the Soldier, Portuguese Joe, and many others.

With its bigger strikes, the community at Mac Mac had grown to about a thousand by the beginning of 1874. It too had its trading stores and drinking dens. Among the latter was a bar run by Herbert Rhodes, the feckless brother of Cecil. He was one of a group of twelve who had arrived at the diggings from Pietermaritzburg and who called themselves the 'Pilgrims', a name which many of the other diggers soon adopted. Rhodes's bar was called the Spotted Dog, and it was notorious for its brawls. Another renowned watering-hole at Mac Mac was Austin's Bar, one of whose stars was the shrewd Hungarian Alois Nellmapius. In a raucous ceremony one night he was given letters patent to the title of Count. Starting as a diggers' joke, the name of 'Count' Nellmapius stuck, and the fake handle proved very useful in smoothing the passage of its bearer's ambitious business deals in the years that followed.

But much of Mac Mac's and Spitskop's vibrant energy was soon to be diverted elsewhere. For in September 1873 a new and incomparably richer field was found.

In that month, a dour Scottish prospector named Alec Patterson decided he had had enough of the area and began to look elsewhere. He had earned himself the nickname of 'Wheelbarrow Alec' from his habit of carrying his gear around in a barrow – unlike the majority of the miners, who bore their worldly possessions on their backs. Patterson finished working out his Mac Mac claim, then quietly loaded his wheelbarrow and set off.

He told no one where he was going. He simply vanished over the ridge above the camp, leaving the other diggers to their labours. Up the steep hill he trundled his barrow, his eyes narrowed for the tell-tale glint in the grass or in a likely-looking stream, and in due course he reached the rim of a valley. Below him a small river wound away to its juncture with the Blyde River, its banks dotted with peach trees. Patterson made his way down, unloaded his wheelbarrow, made his camp on the edge of the creek, and settled down to pan the gravel scooped from below the cool, fresh mountain water. And among the gravel was gold.

Not simply a thin trace, but a rich yield, a payable yield! As far as he could see, the whole stream was filled with it, glinting invitingly among the pebbles, lurking in the shadows under the boulders. It was without doubt the biggest treasure yet found. In short, a fortune. Patterson sat back in a daze on the bank of the stream, seeing his dreams of wealth take solid shape before his eyes.

But after the first excitement, a Caledonian caution set in. The more gold, the more men, he reminded himself. If the news were to leak out, a frantic horde of competing diggers would descend on this sylvan scene. Wheelbarrow Alec had little difficulty in persuading himself to lie low and go on prospecting, undetected, for as long as possible.

But his secret was not to last long. A new figure appeared high in the valley, tracing the Scotsman's trail: William Trafford, a man as voluble as Patterson was taciturn. He soon spotted what Patterson, scowling at him from the creek, was up to. Within moments he was at the same work, and with swift reward. Rising to his feet, he announced joyfully to the high hills: 'The pilgrim is at rest!'

Trafford, of course, lost no time in spreading the wonderful news. In the middle of September he arrived breathlessly at the door of Major MacDonald's tent at Mac Mac to report and register his claims. As the news flashed through the little village, the miners hurriedly gathered up their belongings. With picks and shovels on their backs, they streamed away up the hill and down into the quiet valley with its peach trees. Soon came the sound of iron on stone, the tumbling of boulders, the joyous shouts of discovery, one upon the other, a chorus of jubilation.

The Transvaal's first fully-fledged gold-mining town, Pilgrim's Rest, had been born.

Gold fever

'Here comes another pilgrim to his rest!'

As the tide of hairy humanity swept down on him, Alec Patterson muttered his fierce imprecation. Within a few days some 200 diggers had swarmed in from Mac Mac and Spitskop, including old comrades such as Spanish Joe and the inimitable Matthias Mockett, a 40-year-old ex-sailor known to one and all as 'The Bosun'. And as news of the finds spread, men came from still farther afield. Sailors in the ports jumped their ships to head inland. Kimberley, where many of the diamond claims had been exhausted, provided about a third of the newcomers.

Soon the news reached out beyond the borders of the Transvaal, to Europe and America and to the goldfields of Australia. Infected with the powerful contagion of gold-fever, yet more men took ship for Africa.

Once arrived, they found their way to the diggings by various ways. The two main routes were from Port Natal and Delagoa Bay. That from Port Natal went through Pietermaritzburg, Wakkerstroom and Lydenburg to Pilgrim's Rest. At 800 kilometres, it was the longest but also the safest. Most of those who took this road stocked up in Pietermaritzburg, then went on by horse or ox-cart to the diggings. Along the way they were accommodated in hostelries, which varied from the barely tolerable to abject hovels infested with cockroaches and bedbugs.

Many hopeful diggers, impatient with the tedium of this route, chose the shorter but more hazardous way from Lourenço Marques. They pushed west for 280 kilometres through the marshes, the Lebombo Mountains, and the Lowveld bush to the foothills of the 'Berg. Those fortunate enough to secure transport by ox-wagon had a greater chance of survival than the intrepid spirit who walked. Malaria, yellow-fever and tsetse took their inevitable toll of both man and beast, especially on the first leg of the journey, through the marshes. The swamp had its crocodiles, the dry ground its lions. Many lost their lives without even seeing a gold-bearing stream. Some took bearers with them, but these were notoriously unreliable. They had a tendency to melt into the bush, taking with them the miners' food, belongings and digging equipment. And after all this, there was still the steep face of the 'Berg itself to be climbed.

Despite the high mortality on the way, the village at Pilgrim's Rest continued to grow apace. Three separate camps – the upper, middle and lower – had been established along the banks of the creek. From the beginning, the richest part of the valley was its middle section, that discovered by Alec Patterson. It was here that most of the tents were pitched and the richest claims worked.

Where possible, the digger tried to secure a claim straddling the stream, with a section of bank on either side. This was to gain access to the alluvial gold in the stream itself, but, as important, also to have a supply of water for the process of separating and washing the gold. Each claim measured a standard 150 by 150 Cape feet, and was pegged out with four poles marking each corner and projecting about a metre from the ground. On the pole was a plate or card bearing the owner's name. The claim was his by right and could be worked by no one else, provided he had registered it and paid the monthly five shilling fee at MacDonald's office. In the first months of the new rush this was still at Mac Mac, but early in January 1874 the Commissioner transferred his headquarters to Pilgrim's Rest. At first, as at Mac Mac, his office was in his tent, on the edge of the track which ran parallel to the diggings some seventy metres above the stream, but in due course it was replaced by a shack.

Once the digger had pegged his claim, he began work in earnest. In the early days, the stream itself was panned and yielded a healthy amount of gold. But this soon became exhausted, and the miners turned their attention to the surrounding ground. In the course of ages, the gold carried down by the river from the seams and strata which honeycombed the mountain slopes had sunk through the soil, coming to rest on bedrock. The miner's task was to remove the mass of topsoil, which could be anything up to six metres in depth, to reach the gold-bearing layer of 'wash' over the rock. This herculean task, indeed, occupied a good part of the digger's average day.

It began in the first light of dawn. He had little distance to walk to work, since his tent was usually on or close to his claim. Personal hygiene was probably the least of his preoccupations: washing was cursory, shaving virtually unknown. Indeed, the miner's bushy beard was almost his badge of office. The fire would be stirred to life, and a billycan of water put on to boil. Soon the whole camp would be moving, as the men stretched their stiff muscles for the long day. With twelve hours of back-breaking labour ahead, they ate as heartily as they could. For those with little money, breakfast would consist of mealie-meal washed down with strong, scalding tea. Those in funds, though, would enjoy meat and a welcome tot of rum or brandy.

Then, with pick and shovel, they would attack the heavy red soil, enlarging the scars already cut in the banks of the stream. The biggest obstacles were the boulders, which were both a blessing and a curse. Nuggets and pockets of coarse gold tended to collect around and under them, so they were the focus of particular attention. There was an established procedure for removing a large boulder. First, a hole was dug beside it, then the earth around it loosened until it could be rolled into the hole. In the case of a large rock, this might mean hours, even days, of work. To feel when it was about to descend, a miner would stand barefooted on it, waiting for the first tremor. When this came, he would bellow a warning to those below and spring clear. Unfortunately, this early-warning system was far from infallible, and horrific accidents occurred from time to time. The survivors, however, were often consoled with the finding of splendid nuggets that had been concealed under the rock. These would be lovingly picked up, along with any coarse grains of gold, and stowed in a jar or can, the Colman's mustard tin being a favourite receptacle.

The bulk of the fine gold, however, lay in the wash and rocks directly over the bedrock. This was processed and the gold separated on the edge of the stream in the miner's sluice-box, an essential piece of equipment in the diggings. It consisted of a long trough of wood, supported on trestles. The trough usually measured five to six metres in length, and was about half a metre high and the same in width. At its upper end it would be connected with the stream by a 'water race', which was simply a narrow channel by which the water was led into the box. It could be diverted when necessary and the supply of water thus controlled. At the bottom of the box were wooden slats, fixed crosswise and known as a 'Venetian ripple'. The mixture of earth and stones from the bedrock level of the claim was shovelled into the box with the water from the stream running through it. The gold, heavier than the rest, would sink to the bottom, to be caught in the slats of the Venetian ripple. Where the gold was more than usually fine, it was the practice to line the bottom of the box with a blanket, a sheep-skin or ox-hide, in the hairs of which the fine particles would collect.

This labour went on through the day, with a break of an hour at

The middle years. The halcyon days
of the lone pick-and-shovel digger of
the Pilgrim's Rest area were short-
lived: by 1875 the easily-accessible
gold deposits were virtually
exhausted, and the era of the small-
workings gave way to that of the
bigger mines, ones with capital,
machinery and technical expertise.
Clockwise from left: underground
drilling in one of the Transvaal Gold
Mining Exploration Company's
shafts; the Vaalhoek Mine in its
heyday; cocopans on the railway
line, built in the early years of the
century; crushing mills at Brown's
Hill. *Above:* transporting gold-
bearing ore by cableway.

33

noon for rest. Sundown was the moment the miner looked forward to. This was when he 'cleaned up'. The water from the sluice-box would be diverted back into the stream, to expose the mush of gold and gravel at the bottom of the box, which would be carefully scraped out and panned in the stream, in an iron pan, about forty centimetres across. The pan was filled with water, which was swirled and shaken to wash away the mud and pebbles, leaving a deposit of gold as the day's reward. The yield might be a fine 'tail', little more than a trace – amounting to a couple of pennyweights – or on a good day to as much as eight ounces. And, of course, there were the bonanza days when the miner struck it rich with a pan heavy with 'ash-blond' gold. It was these 'clean-ups' which kept the miner's hopes alive through the long hours of sweated labour in sun and rain. It was always a gamble, for in the jumbled geology of the region the patterns – in the distribution of alluvial gold – could not be clearly discerned. One man might wash tons of earth, working through several claims, without finding a single ounce, while his neighbour might fill his jar with nuggets and dust in a few hours.

As the day's work drew to a close, the miners of Pilgrim's Rest, as at Mac Mac and Spitskop, homed in on the camp's social centres – the canteens.

It was rumoured that the real fortunes in Pilgrim's Rest were made in these places, though competition was stiff. By October 1874 there were eighteen in the village, all purveying the diggers' favourite brews: Cape brandy and Squareface gin. As at Mac Mac, many of the dens bore original and raffish names. Most were congregated in the wealthy middle stretch of the creek, where Tom Craddock kept his famous bar. Here, too were Ye Digger's Bar and the Halfway House. Even more renowned, or perhaps notorious, was the tarpaulin-roofed mud building belonging to one Stent, known universally as 'Stent's Cathedral'. Farther down, at the juncture of Pilgrim's Creek and the Blyde River, was the tent-bar, Our House, owned by Yorkie the Yorkshireman.

Into these places, a twelve-hour thirst hard upon them, swarmed the motley crew of diggers. They usually paid for the drinks in the only currency available: gold dust. An ounce in the early days was worth about £3. 10s. while a pennyweight fetched between 3s. 6d. and 3s. 9d. A bottle of gin retailed at a little under two pennyweights, and a bottle of Cape brandy at slightly more. The traders and barmen all kept scales on their counters. The customer would sprinkle the gold from his tin or jar until the balance tipped. Understandably, a great care was taken in the weighing. The barman reserved the right to 'blow' the gold, gently puffing on it to remove any dust which might add a fraction to its weight. Since this was laborious and took up precious drinking time, many of the miners came to an arrangement with the bar-owner. They would hand over their week's takings, to be used as credit for the following week. As a general policy, when they made a find many of the men drank steadily until their money ran out. Then, somewhat less steadily, they returned to their claims, to have their credit restored by a dint of good, hard labour in the fresh air.

Deep poverty existed next to eruptions of sudden wealth. In the early days in particular, while there were still many fine nuggets to be found on or near the surface, men made fortunes. Three partners, Messrs Barrington, Osborne and Farley, for example, picked up 13 lb. 8oz. of gold in nugget form in one day. Another partnership of four netted £35 000 for each man before they had exhausted their claim. But if quickly earned, a fortune could equally quickly be squandered, and often was. Even those who had made enough money to leave found it hard to tear themselves away from the hope and excitement of further search, compulsively spending their gains, living and dying on their butchered patch of land.

Around these people, the confirmed and habitual prospectors, a strange society grew up, with its own codes and customs. While it was generally a law-abiding community – compared for example with the rough-house conditions in the American and Australian goldfields – there was inevitable friction, provoked largely by isolation and by overcrowding. By early January 1874, when MacDonald moved to the camp, there were already 1 500 diggers working the area. Regulations governing conduct were laid down by a Diggers' Committee. Many of the rules derived from tradition and common consent. One of them, borrowed from the Californian fields, specified the ending of the working day, at five or six o'clock in the evening: any man labouring at night would be suspected of stealing a march on his comrades, and was subject to a fine of £5 or more. There was no appeal against the Committee's decision. Likewise, Sunday was proclaimed a day of rest. The invisible boundaries of the claims as defined by the pegs were sacrosanct, and there were few cases of claim-jumping at Pilgrim's Rest.

The most powerful taboo was that on the theft of gold. On the rare occasions when a man's gold was stolen and the culprit found, punishment was swift and harsh. Lashes, beard-cropping, and exile from the camp were the normal penalty. For other, lesser offences, the village gaol sufficed – more or less. The first prison was a bell-tent which, naturally, required the co-operation of its inmate. It was soon replaced by a wattle-and-daub hut that was only slightly more secure, so by agreement the prisoners were released between sunrise and sunset to work their claims and placed on their honour to return to gaol at night.

Apart from their heroic binges, the miners lived frugally. In the days before imported prefabricated shacks, most of them slept in tents, either the bell-type with a central pole, or square tents with a second canvas at the top to allow for ventilation. Home-made tents of this kind could be bought for 30 shillings, and a thriving trade grew up around them. Only when a payable claim had been struck would a miner think of building a more permanent structure – usually one of mud-brick with a grass roof on the tribal pattern. A variation was the so-called 'cap-style' of house. This comprised a single room with very low clay walls, covered with a high, pointed grass roof. It had a door at the front and a single small window at the rear. Again, after the tribal fashion, many of the miners built separate cooking huts, usually little more than a few poles supporting a grass roof. A digger lucky enough to own a wagon slept under its canvas.

Furniture was, at best, stark and functional. Most utensils were of tin, and each tent had its supply of tin mugs, plates and pails. The men cooked their simple fare in three-legged black iron pots and brewed tea and coffee in heavy iron kettles. Packing cases served as tables and chairs. And, of course, a keg of hard tack was *de rigueur* in every digger's home. Liquor flowed freely enough, but generally speaking food was scarce. The few local farmers supplied the only provisions, the bulk of it comprising mealie-meal, and prices were high. A bag of meal for baking, for example, cost in the region of 60 to 80 shillings. A 68 kilogram sack of potatoes fetched 40 shillings, a pound of butter cost 3s. 6d., and a tin of condensed milk 2s. 6d.

Besides gold and liquor, there were other ways of making a living in the camp. One of these was to traffic in water. Essential as it was to the whole process of washing and panning the gold, the supply became heavily over-used as more and more diggers arrived. It remained clear enough at the top of the valley, but by the time it reached the Blyde River at the bottom it had turned into a thick brown ooze. Soon water became almost as precious as the gold itself. In response to rising demand, a number of enterprising souls abandoned unprofitable claims and went into the water supply business, digging long races from streams often many kilometres away. Verona's race, for instance, carried water for 15 kilometres along the contours of the hills and down into the valley. There, the rights to its usage were leased by the day.

Within the community were men with special skills, including a number of doctors. In general, they were more interested in gold than in treating the sick and saving lives. One at least, though, was a serious medical practitioner, an easy-going Lancashire man named James Edward Ashton. He set up his practice in a tent, with a large sign outside declaring him 'Surgeon, Barber and Tentmaker'. To cope with emergencies, the diggers themselves organized a small, voluntarily-run hospital, in a tent containing a few beds and comforts. Once a week the medical officer of the Lydenburg district paid a visit, and the diggers took turns to serve as hospital orderlies. Their ministrations, it was reported, were willing if somewhat rough.

Among other refinements to appear in Pilgrim's Rest was a newspaper, started by the excitable and polemical Irishman W. J. Phelan. The *Gold News*, whose first issue went on sale on 28 January 1874, couched in the diggers' own salty language, was scurrilous in tone and openly, even violently, partisan. Not surprisingly, like many journalists of the day, Phelan took the precaution of keeping a pair of loaded pistols in his desk and a burly bodyguard lounging in the front office!

In these overcrowded and isolated conditions, there was a degree of unrest among the diggers, similar to that which had occurred at Mac Mac. In particular, they felt that they were being ignored by the government. On 12 January, 1874, MacDonald wrote to the Volksraad at Pretoria to complain that he was having trouble with the latest arrivals, who were proving difficult to control. In reply, the State Secretary informed the Gold Commissioner that President Burgers himself would pay a visit to the camp early in February.

There was, though, another motive for Burgers's visit. Despite its healthier credit rating, the Republic's acute financial malaise had not been cured by the discovery of gold. The Transvaal still owed the Cape Commercial Bank £60 000. Burgers himself had ambitious plans to improve his country's threadbare education system, and to build a railway line to Lourenço Marques. The old 'bluebacks' were being called in, but the new note issue was scarcely more popular. The miners themselves showed a sublime indifference to paper currency: all their dealings were in gold, and though many squandered their wealth there were many others who hoarded their nuggets against the time when they would leave the area. To this day it remains uncertain how much gold was really mined at Pilgrim's Rest, or how much was quietly spirited away, to be sold in Lourenço Marques, Natal or Cape Town, where the buyers were making 10s. to 15s. an ounce on the transactions.

Burgers urgently needed to keep the Transvaal's wealth within the national borders, and he had a scheme: to buy gold in Pilgrim's Rest and to have it minted into coins of the realm, the first currency of its kind in the Republic. He had put the idea to his Executive Council, gained its approval, and was allowed funds with which to buy the gold. Curiously, though, he refrained from consulting the Volksraad on the matter, deciding instead to announce it as a *fait accompli*, at the opening of the next session, due to begin in May.

First, however, the matter of the miners' unrest had to be resolved. Punctually on 2 February, Burgers arrived for his second visit to a gold-mining camp.

The Presidential wagon rumbled down into the valley of the Blyde River – but there it encountered an obstacle, for it had rained heavily over the previous few days and the river was swollen in flood. On the far side was assembled a mutinous-looking crowd of miners, their beards bristling in anticipation of a good quarrel. Somewhat nervously, the Presidential party stopped for a council of war. Then one of their number, H. W. Struben, took charge of the situation: he stripped off his clothes and swam across the river. A curious scene followed as the naked, dripping Struben expostulated with the men. He told them Burgers had come to talk, and to listen to their problems. This piece of unorthodox diplomacy succeeded well enough, and tempers cooled.

But the river still had to be negotiated. A long rope was brought from the camp, and Struben swam back across with it. Then the diggers hauled the wagon, with Burgers seated precariously aboard, across the flood. It was a tense moment for the President: he later confessed to Struben that he couldn't swim!

Once safely on the opposite bank, the two sides conferred, very much as they had done the year before at Mac Mac. And again Burgers managed to smooth the prospectors' ruffled feathers before going on to discuss the introduction of new mining laws. The climax of the day was the picnic banquet laid on for the President at the camp. It was lubricated with copious draughts of champagne, and long remembered by those present. The Bosun – Matthias Mockett – who was in charge of the menu, turned out a plum duff, liberally doused with his own recipe for a brandy sauce, for the final course. The normally abstemious President, far from his worries in Pretoria, seems to have succumbed to the warmth and *bonhomie* of the occasion. He even asked for a second helping of the duff with a double ration of its intoxicating sauce, though he rather spoiled the effect by also requesting a chisel with which to cut The Bosun's pastry! He was somewhat dismayed, though, by the quantity of gin and brandy as well as champagne which flowed around him as the afternoon wore on. When taxed on this, the resourceful Mockett laid the blame squarely on the diggers' upbringing. 'It weren't their fault,' he confided, 'their mothers taught them to drink!' When this line failed to impress his guest, he appealed to higher authority. Thrusting his ample miner's beard close to the startled Burgers, he intoned a quotation from Timothy 5:23 'Drink no longer water but take a little wine for thy stomach's sake'!

But Burgers had not forgotten the main purpose of his visit. In the next few days he set about acquiring gold for the coins he planned. Somewhat surprisingly, he received some expert advice from one of the non-digging inhabitants of Pilgrim's Rest, a Swiss immigrant named Perrin who had worked in his country's State Mint before coming to the Transvaal, where he had applied for a licence as an assayer. He had then moved to Pilgrim's Rest, where he compiled an eleven-page memorandum advising the South African Republic to start a mint at the new settlement, to the benefit, he felt, of all. 'Should the government,' he wrote, 'give to the digger the intermediary price between the real value of the finds and the amount offered to him by any other purchaser, the bargain would still be a very remunerative one for both contractors. The price of gold increasing would soon prove an encouragement for all hands at work already, an effective allurement for many yet to come.'

Here was confirmation of many of Burgers's own convictions. Perrin presented his document to the President, who studied it at length a few days after his arrival in the camp. Soon Burgers was busy buying gold. Though it is uncertain exactly how much he acquired, it is known that he gave MacDonald £1 000 with instructions to purchase the metal, and he himself bought two large nuggets. Then, on 9 February, he wrote a letter, headed 'Pilgrim's Rest, New Caledonia', to J. J. Pratt, the South African Republic's Consul-General in London, informing his diplomatic representative that 'the Government having resolved to get a few coins struck to the value of the English sovereigns, I have bought 300 oz. of our Native gold for that purpose which I shall remit to you immediately on my return to Pretoria. The Assembly will meet in May next and by that time I am anxious to have the money here. As the time is short I write to you about the matter in

Early diggers' tents dot the lovely countryside around 'The Creek' at Pilgrim's Rest. There were in fact three separate camps along the watercourse: the upper, middle and lower, the middle section proving the most rewarding. But most of the real fortunes of the early days were made in the social centres – the canvas-and-packing-case canteens of Spitzkop, Mac Mac and Pilgrim's Rest. By October 1872, a few months after the first big gold find, there were fully eighteen drinking-places in Pilgrim's Rest alone, each trading their Cape brandy and Squareface gin for the diggers' hard-earned gold dust.

time to make enquiries either at the Royal Mint in London or at some other mint in Belgium or elsewhere, whether there is a chance of getting the work executed in time'. For 'Government', of course, read Burgers himself.

His visit to Pilgrim's Rest concluded and the gold secured, the President bade farewell to the miners and returned to Pretoria. A few days later the State Secretary wrote to Pratt from the capital to inform him that the gold was on its way. He added details of what was required for the coins:

'I also send you a portrait of His Honour the President and a sketch of the way in which the sovereigns are to be struck. They must have the exact value of the British £1 sterling. I enclose several copies of our Coat of Arms. By a mistake of the printer the word Transvaal has been put between the S.A. Republic. I have drawn a line through it as it must not be inserted but the words Zuid-Afrikaansche Republiek must be so divided that they just fill the circle round our Coat of Arms. The President is very anxious to have the coins here in Pretoria at the commencement of May, so no time must be lost. Please have the dies prepared at once so that when the gold has arrived you can have the coins struck.'

Twenty-two and a quarter pounds of gold in raw state were sent to London. There, Pratt consulted the Royal Mint and a number of assayers, and discovered that there was no hope whatsoever of having the sovereigns minted in time for the May deadline. However, he found an engraver to the Royal Mint named L. C. Wyon, who was prepared to make the necessary dies and punches for the modest fee of £42. In the meantime, Messrs Johnson, Matthey & Co of Hatton Gardens had been called in to alloy the gold with a one-twelfth part of copper – the British standard. Messrs Heaton & Son of Birmingham, a firm of 'moneyers' – authorized manufacturers of coins and medals – agreed to make the sovereigns at 3d each, using the dies, punches and gold supplied. There was a last-minute hitch caused by a 'breakdown' of the dies, resulting in the two slightly different designs recognized by experts: the 'thick beard' and 'thin beard' Burgers sovereigns.

A total of 837 coins was minted. By special permission of the President, Pratt was allowed to keep four. The remaining 833 coins were dispatched to the Transvaal, followed by an account for £90. 0s. 10d. It was not until 24 September, 1874, when the next session of the Transvaal Volksraad convened, that Burgers was able to announce that he had sent gold from the Pilgrim's Rest area to Britain to be minted into coins to the value of £1 000, and to show the Raad's members £50-worth of samples.

The news was welcomed with prolonged and hearty applause. It was, Burgers said, a great step forward in the forming of a nation. This gained him renewed applause. Then he added that his own likeness had been engraved on the coins, though this had been strictly against his wishes, and gained no applause at all. This was, members felt, hardly in accord with the republican spirit, and soon probing questions were being directed at the President. He had committed two serious errors: he had failed to consult the Volksraad beforehand, and, worse, he had allowed, if not caused, a 'graven image' of himself to appear on the coins. This was altogether too imperial a gesture for the Volksraad, and the heated debate continued through the following day. Eventually, five motions were put to the vote, four of them rejecting the coinage as legal tender. Rejection, though, would mean the loss of a very substantial £800, which the country could ill afford, and realization of this prompted an about-face. A fresh motion was proposed and accepted:

'The Raad resolves to accept the gold pieces which were laid before it by His Honour the State President and declared by His Honour to be of the exact and same value as one English pound sterling, as legal tender in this Republic.'

Informed of the Raad's decision, Burgers graciously thanked Members, repeating that he had not had the coins struck for his own glory, but that of the country. There would be more minted, he promised, including others of lesser value. The next day, he ceremoniously handed 24 of the coins to the Chairman. Each member received a coin in token of his first day's attendance at the Raad session for that year. The President decreed that the new coinage would be named the 'staatspond', the word 'sovereign' being obviously inappropriate in a republic. The Raad wound off the occasion by presenting one of the new coins to Burgers as a memento of the solemn moment.

Some 700 staatsponden eventually found their way into general circulation. They were eagerly snapped up, and within a few days were worth £2 apiece. Today they are collector's items, featuring among the rarest and most prized of the country's coins. In due course, after the discovery of gold on the Witwatersrand, a State Mint was established in Pretoria. There, for a few months before the outbreak of the Boer War, the Swiss assayer, Perrin, served as Master of the Mint. But no further coins bearing Burgers's beard, thick or thin, were ever minted. Meanwhile, having made their contribution to local numismatic history, the miners of Pilgrim's Rest went on with their ever-hopeful search for wealth.

Canvas, dirt and water

For the pick-and-shovel miner, the high point of the alluvial diggings at Pilgrim's Rest was the two years following the first strikes: from 1873 to 1875. In that short space of time many diggers, using the simplest of methods, made fortunes. This period also yielded a rich fund of stories and legends, reflecting the eccentricities of this polyglot society of men from all corners of the earth.

A cheerful mixture of accents and tongues, from Cockney to Australian, from American to Irish, from French and German to Polish and Swedish, contributed to the vivid tapestry of pioneer life. In the lists of diggers registered in the Gold Commissioner's office there were many names reflecting this diversity of origin, men such as French Bob and German George, Spanish Joe and Yankee Dan. Others were a carry-over from former professions: The Bosun; Sailor Harry; Charlie the Reefer; Wally the Soldier. Yet others, such as Artful Joe, combined an explicit character and, sometimes, an implicit warning. Among those who kept their own surnames and were buried with them were men who stood out as leaders and spokesmen, men such as Wild Bill Leathern, Bill McPherson, Jimmy Bryson and Alick Dempster, Billy Dawkins and Ted Sievewright (immortalized in the pages of *Jock of the Bushveld*).

They left their names in the record, and some added theirs to the map. Again, these often reflected origins or experience. A myriad creeks (running spruits) and gulches (dry spruits), ridges and gullies dot the area. The American connection persists, for instance, in Sacramento Creek and Klondyke Creek. A strip of land called Baker's Bliss commemorates the luck of a London dentist who came to the Transvaal to pull teeth but ended up digging for gold. If spruits became creeks, koppies became hills – Brown's Hill and Columbia Hill, Walker's Hill and Black Hill.

To pay for the basics of life, a miner had to find an ounce of gold a week. Those who dropped below the subsistence level often kept themselves alive by selling their labour. They worked other men's claims for the accepted wage of £3. 10s. a week. Many of even the poorest, though, would keep a two-ounce nugget stowed safely away – to pay for burial and a headstone in the event of untimely death.

At first, the white diggers themselves provided most of the labour. But this soon changed. Miners from Kimberley, where black labour had long been used, looked askance on the Englishmen and Americans who did their own manual work. Among those who agreed with the locals was Alois Nellmapius, the 'Count' from Mac Mac, now settled at Pilgrim's Rest. His sharp nose had quickly led him to payable gold, but equally quickly he had tired of digging. It wasn't long before he had hired a gang of the Pedi tribesmen and, having delivered a brief lecture on the art of using pick and shovel, set them to work, for nominal wages plus a supply of mealie-meal. Almost overnight, Nellmapius's claim doubled its productivity, and the other miners hurried to follow his capitalist example.

The black workers had their female counterparts in the flock of 'cooks' and 'housekeepers' who made their appearance. These women, if not technically slaves, were in reality little more. They were brought by Portuguese traders from Lourenço Marques, and 'sold' to the diggers. They quickly settled in, and soon there was a growing population of small brown children roaming the camp.

Creature comforts of a more orthodox kind were provided by the first white women to make their way to the diggings. Some of them, a minority, arrived as wives of the miners. Mrs Tom McLachlan had already settled with her husband on the farm Geelhoutboom at Mac Mac, where she did much to improve the dig-

gers' standards of health and hygiene. One of the first to reach Pilgrim's Rest and leave a record of her impressions was a Mrs MacDonald. Her view was somewhat jaundiced:

'The gold fields offer a peculiar scene, as if some volcanic action had taken place. Diggers' tents dotted about, some at the bottom of the diggings 200 to 300 feet deep, and seemingly in the very bowels of the earth, some perched on top of a precipice, and the long sluice boxes which carry the water to wash the gold, all tend to blend into an incongruous mass of canvas, boulders, dirt and water, all together.'

She described the sorry state of the camp in the wet season when rain, lightning and wind combined to wreak havoc on the vulnerable tents and wagons, and everybody and everything was left covered in a thick coating of red mud. She also noted the chronic shortage of food, adding a moral footnote: 'It is now that I see that gold will not buy anything, for it cannot buy food.'

The weather in fact could produce some astonishing surprises. Among these was an extraordinary event which took place in 1875, a bizarre accident of nature recorded by a certain Dr Atcherley in his book, *A Trip to Boer Land*, in which he wrote:

'A very heavy rainfall had taken place, accompanied by one of those fearful thunderstorms so frequent in these latitudes. The quiet creek was converted into a roaring torrent which was rolling boulders along like wisps of straw. The terrified inhabitants of the camp stood by horror-stricken, watching the destruction, when by some marvel, and without sign of warning, the boiling flood suddenly ceased and where, a moment before, an enormous volume of water had been rushing by, an insignificant rivulet now trickled lazily along.'

It appeared that the weight of the water had opened up a fissure in the bed of the creek, giving access to one of the multitude of subterranean passages in the mountain. The river was simply diverted headlong into this chasm. The next morning, when the flood had abated, the miners set to work and diverted the stream to expose the mouth of the crevice. Beams were laid across it, and a man carrying a torch was gingerly lowered on a rope into the yawning darkness below, He went down some ninety feet, and was then hauled back up to the surface, emerging pale and shaken into the sunlight. He reported that he had heard rushing water and the 'crashing of rocks' but had been unable to see the bottom of the cavern. Then a weight was lowered on a plumb-line, finally touching the bottom at 200 feet. Awed, the miners quickly covered up the mouth of the fissure with stone-work, channelled the river back over it, and returned to the more familiar and profitable pursuit of gold.

Not all the women were as disapproving as Mrs MacDonald. Among the first to arrive in the early 1870s was Miss Elizabeth Russell, a character as intrepid as any on the diggings. She was the daughter of a Pretoria shopkeeper, raised with customary Victorian decorum to become, in due course, a schoolmistress in the Orange Free State. But she had dreams, and an adventurous spirit. With her younger brother as chaperon, she commandeered an ox-wagon, and, to the anger and dismay of her father, set out for Pilgrim's Rest. The ride, lasting a bumpy six weeks, was the usual mixture of dust and discomfort. Indeed, at one point, the driver of the wagon made a bid to turn back, only to be held to his duty by the determined Miss Russell.

When she finally rolled through the Blyde River and into Pilgrim's Rest, a near-riot broke out in the valley. The vision of a white woman, and a young one at that, was almost more than manly flesh could bear. But Elizabeth, serenely impervious to the shock-waves she had caused, calmly put up her tent, pegged out a claim for herself, registered it at MacDonald's office, and then pitched in with the best. With two African workers, in wind, rain and sun, sometimes up to her knees in water, she worked her claim. Indeed she worked a number of claims, before hitting on a profitable deposit. Besides digging and panning by day, she also found the time and energy to bring a modicum of style to Pilgrim's Rest. The burly, bearded miners must have been both amused and impressed when Miss Russell erected a fence around her tent and planted herself a vegetable patch. Within a short time she had the best-tended site in the camp, a veritable home-from-home in which she made her own ginger beer and pastries, which she sold to the diggers. These luxuries were in great demand, for they made a welcome change from the normally spartan fare.

Among the visitors to Miss Russell's tent was the Reverend Cawkill Barker, an Anglican parson in whom the Demon Drink had pegged out a claim. It seems he had been exiled to Pilgrim's Rest by his superiors in staid Pretoria, where his drinking had made him an embarrassment. In the camp, he made a regular habit of calling on Elizabeth in her tent, the pleasure of her company being diminished only a little by the effort of drinking her lukewarm ginger beer. It is said that the Gold Commissioner, hearing of these visits, made a sardonic remark about what would have been their real purpose. When this salacious inference reached her ears, Elizabeth hitched up her skirts, marched off to find the Commissioner, and laid into him with a horsewhip. Given MacDonald's 'Wild West' origins, it is unlikely she did him any grave injury, but at least she made her point.

Among the men in the camp, marital competition for the few white women was fierce. Elizabeth herself inspired a notable if somewhat delayed contretemps when she married, in December 1874, a digger named Cameron. The wedding took place in Miss Russell's home-town of Pretoria, after which the happy couple returned to the diggings, where they were given a reception banquet on the miners' usual lavish scale. The occasion was marred, however, by one of Elizabeth's rejected suitors, who, in a fit of jealousy, smote the bride from behind with a hob-nailed boot, knocking her over, finery and all. The bridegroom rose manfully to the challenge, peeled off his coat and thrashed the offender on the spot. Justice effected, the party went on its swinging way deep into the night.

This was not of course the only instance of a rift over a woman. Another incident of the time, related thirty years later in the *Mines and Claim-Holders Journal*, arose from friction between two diggers, Jimmy Bryson and a man named Smith, who were conducting parallel courtship of 'two attractive and well-built sisters who assisted in a relative's store up the Creek. In the romantic interior of the store Love's young dream stirred the sleeping passion of their souls. The sardine tins beamed a bright approval, the bags of coffee offered aromatic incense, the tins of salmon blushed a deeper pink at little love episodes. Here were two bachelors of equal degree and two maidens of equal charm. Surely on this occasion the course of true love might have run smooth?'

Far from it. One afternoon a group of diggers, including The Bosun, who later attested to the full story, wandered into the store. There, they found the two suitors gripped in 'an almighty tussle' on the floor. They were pulled apart, and one of the onlookers suggested they settle their differences in more formal fashion.

A duel was agreed; seconds appointed, two rifles found, and coffee for one prepared the next morning. An excited throng gathered in a secluded corner of the camp.

There, the contestants faced each other, a hundred paces apart. Smith was deeply moved at this moment of destiny by the

conduct of his second, Jimmy MacDonald, who refused to move away from his principal, sharing the risk by standing close behind.

At a given signal, both men fired. The two shots rang out simultaneously. Smith collapsed in a welter of blood.

Bryson's second abandoned his man and rushed across the clearing to where the others were gathered around the fallen protagonist. Then he turned and shouted back at the waxen-faced victor: 'For God's sake clear off, Bryson. He's done for!'

Bryson needed no further prompting. With a despairing wave of the hand he disappeared into the bush at speed.

Smith, however, was far from dead. Indeed he was not even injured – he was suffering from severe shock, and had fainted dead away. He was carried into a nearby hut, where he revived enough to be given the real story by MacDonald and his accomplices. The rifles had been loaded with blank cartridges, and the blood came from a blood-filled sheep's bladder which, at the moment of firing, MacDonald had clapped down over his principal's head.

Needless to say the humour of this denouement was largely lost on Smith. It was some time before he could be persuaded that he was still in the land of the living, that he was not fatally wounded, and that the story was not a confection to ease his dying moments. He stayed in his bed for a further two weeks before he felt well enough to rise, during which time the conspirators were obliged to work his claim for him.

Meanwhile the terrified Bryson, with the vision of Judge Lynch looming over him, remained up in the hills above Pilgrim's Rest. It took the now-chastened MacDonald several forays to find the man and persuade him that no noose awaited him on his return to civilization. The opinion of the prime movers of this episode – the two damsels in the store – is not recorded. The miners liked their jokes, like their drink, to be strong.

Given the almost universal worship of Mammon, it is surprising to note that any other deity ever made headway at Pilgrim's Rest. But side by side with the canteens, the Gold Commissioner's office and the first bank stood the first church. Like the others, it began humbly, in a tent. It was run by the Reverend Blencowe, a Methodist minister who arrived, accompanied by his wife, in 1874. Blencowe was not short of raw material for his sermons, though how effective they were is debatable. Temperance fought a rearguard action at Pilgrim's Rest, and the Golden Calf was quite literally at hand. But if religion hardly flourished, it did make steady progress: a few years later a four-square wattle-and-daub church made its appearance.

Behind the building, on the steep, sun-smitten flank of the hill, was the town graveyard. Like so much else in this valley, it came about by chance. On the face of it this is an unlikely place for a cemetery: the winding path up from the church is narrow and, for pall-bearers, tortuously difficult to negotiate. The earliest marked grave is that of Joseph Lord, who was buried in March 1873, six months after the rush to the valley began, but there were already other, unmarked, graves on the site before Lord was buried. One of the village's most treasured legends recounts their origins.

In the early days of the settlement, a man was caught stealing gold from a tent. Since tent-robbery was regarded by the diggers as among the most heinous of crimes, the man was lucky to escape with his life. Instead, he was told to disappear, and warned that if he ever returned he would be shot. But a few days later the thief decided, foolishly, to put goldfields justice to the test. He returned to Pilgrim's Rest, where he was promptly gunned down on the hillside, to be buried where he fell. Coincidentally, two more men died shortly afterwards, and were buried nearby, so creating the nucleus of the cemetery. Today the 'Robber's Grave' may still be seen. It is easily recognized, for it is the only one pointing north-east, at right angles to the other graves. Branded a thief in life, the robber remained an exile in death.

If death was a commonplace event in the camp, birth was something of a novelty. John Purcell and his wife, Mary Anne, came from Kimberley, settling first in Mac Mac at the beginning of 1873, then moving on to Pilgrim's Rest. There, on 25 August, 1874, Mary Anne Purcell gave birth to her 'ten-pound nugget', a baby girl christened Maud Mary. The diggers flocked to examine the first white child to be born in the village. As she grew up she became a kind of mascot of the camp, and the miners, so many of whom had left behind home and family, spoiled her shamelessly.

Though the camp was an isolated place, some communication with the outside world – in the form of regular transport services – began in 1874. The first of these was initiated by Pearse, one of the village doctors. He suggested to one of the diggers, Wild Bill Leathern, that he buy a wagonette and horses and start a weekend service between Pilgrim's Rest and Lydenburg. Pearse agreed to pay for the wagon, which could seat about seventeen people. The venture was an immediate success. Leathern would start out on the 60-kilometre journey soon after noon on Saturday. There was no fixed fare: he simply passed his hat around, boasting as he did so that he never left a passenger stranded in Lydenburg. There was an element of friendly blackmail in this, for the weekend would be spent in the bars in Lydenburg, and Leathern would devote his Sunday afternoon to rounding up drunken diggers from the various establishments and returning seventeen hangovers home in the declining hours of Sunday evening. The threat of being 'forgotten' in the round-up was enough to persuade the passengers to donate generously to Leathern's hat!

Encouraged by the success of his first venture, Leathern soon broadened his scope. In May 1874, in partnership with one P. F. Henderson, he started a regular post-cart and passenger service between the goldfields and the Natal border at Wakkerstroom. The carts had accommodation for six persons, who paid £8. 10s. for an agonizing three-day journey. Not surprisingly the number of passengers was small, but the service at least provided contact with the outside world and regular postal communication.

A year after Leathern's enterprise began, a still more ambitious passenger service was launched, by a man with the resounding name of Chevalier Oscar Wilhelm Alric Forssman. He already ran a coach service, called The Transvaal and Goldfields Extension Transport Company, which shuttled between Potchefstroom and the diamond fields of Kimberley. Then the Transvaal Volksraad

offered him a substantial sum (as was so often the case with that body's promises, the money was never paid) to extend his service to Lydenburg. Though the Volksraad did not honour the agreement, Forssman began an eastern service, using a light wagonette drawn by eight horses. The journey from Potchefstroom to Lydenburg, which took a hundred hours, demanded the utmost patience and fortitude from passengers and driver alike.

But if these services brought a welcome breath of the outside world into the camp, there were other reminders of it which were less welcome. Among these were the new gold mining laws, promulgated by the Transvaal Volksraad. In mid-1875 President Burgers, who had long enjoyed the confidence of the diggers (if not of his own people), was away in Europe, attempting to raise a loan for his cherished dream of a railway linking Pretoria and Lourenço Marques. In his absence the Volksraad took the opportunity to propose an increase in the licence fee for claims – from five shillings to ten shillings. The Raad also initiated changes in the regulations governing the granting of block claims, in particular to associations or companies of miners, who would be given exclusive rights to the working of the ground.

The first of these proposals pleased no one. When he learned of it, MacDonald, the Gold Commissioner, forthrightly told the men in Pretoria that, if passed, the measure would trigger serious trouble among the diggers. The second, that governing the granting of blocks of claims, evoked a more complex reaction, one which reflected important changes in the life-style of the miners at Pilgrim's Rest.

For in the first two years the immediately accessible alluvial gold in the valley – that within reach of the limited means of the individual digger – had been virtually exhausted. At the same time, new methods of reaching deeper seams, 'leaders' and deposits, were being developed. These, however, required the combined resources and capital of groups of men or companies. From the beginning there had been those who chose to work together in partnerships, usually of no more than three or four, sharing outlay, work, responsibility and reward. The earliest known partnership to give itself a name was the 'Pilgrim's Rest Gold Fields Company', though it was never registered as such.

With the exhaustion of the surface deposits, the companies began to assume an increasing importance. They represented a new voice in the community, that of the 'capitalist' party, and they challenged the free enterprise convictions of the individual

The gold coach leaving turn-of-the-century Pilgrim's Rest. The first transport service linking the village to the world beyond was started by one Wild Bill Leathern as early as 1874. His single wagon carried seventeen usually-sober diggers to the taverns of Lydenburg, 60 kilometres away, for the weekend. Payment of the fare was 'voluntary', but since Leathern undertook to round up the merrymakers on Sunday afternoon and see them safely home, the cash contributions tended to be generous – an insurance against being 'forgotten' – and the service proved an immediate financial success.

miners. Prominent among the company men was Alois Nellmapius, busy at this time trying to amalgamate a number of claims. He led the faction which supported the Volksraad's proposal to grant exclusive rights to blocks of claims, believing that this was the only way in which goldfields could be properly developed. To this the 'free enterprise' party objected strenuously, claiming that the clause deprived them of the rights granted to them by President Burgers. They also suspected MacDonald of favouring the 'capitalists', and angry petitions demanding his removal from office were sent to Pretoria. MacDonald was already somewhat in disfavour because of his haphazard accounts and his administrative methods which, even by the standards of Pilgrim's Rest, were unorthodox.

There followed a long and bitter exchange of letters between the goldfields and Pretoria, and a positive flood of petitions. But the conservative members of the Volksraad had already made up their minds. Burgers's liberal methods had brought in no revenue from the goldfields; the miners, the 'Engelse', as the Volksraad collectively thought of them, were living at the expense of the Republic; it was time to impose a new order on this unruly crowd. Accordingly, on 21 June, 1875, the new gold law was enacted without amendment.

The measure proved short-lived: the diggers flatly refused to pay the licence fee. The camp seethed with argument; anger threatened to erupt into violence, and MacDonald was forced to put 110 men under 'tent-arrest'. Tension mounted dangerously, and there was a further exchange of correspondence. Faced with a united and adamant digger population, the Volksraad had second thoughts and climbed down; the regulation was amended, and the licence fee reverted to five shillings.

By now, though, MacDonald had wearied of his rôle as principal character in the turbulent drama. As the disturbance subsided, he resigned his post as Gold Commissioner, which had in any case been summarily thrust upon him in the first place. He was given the usual grand banquet by the diggers, and all seems to have been forgiven by the time he set off for Lourenço Marques. It was afterwards found that there was a discrepancy of £240 in his favour in the books. Since the Republic's officials had had ample time in which to discover this before he left, it is to be assumed that they let it stand for services rendered – after all, his had been a chance appointment, and they had done well enough out of him.

Word that the diggers were up 'in revolt' against the government reached Europe in a much exaggerated form just as Burgers was engaged in delicate negotiations for his £300 000 railway loan. Needless to say, the news scarcely helped his case. Nor was it the only setback. By now, the Republic was again on the verge of financial ruin. Sensing his moment, the Pedi chief, Sekhukhune, who had succeeded his father Sekwati in September 1861, formed an alliance with his half-brother Johannes Dinkwayane and began to terrorize the farmers in the Lydenburg district.

With the future of his loan hanging in the balance, President Burgers could not afford a tribal uprising; a prolonged war, or even a less serious engagement, would stretch the Republic's already strained exchequer. On his return to Pretoria he assembled a commando, which he led into Sekhukhune's territory. But Burgers's men had scant faith in his military leadership, and the campaign turned into a disaster. True, there were some initial, minor, successes, but when the commando attacked Sekhukhune's stronghold it was decisively repulsed. Disheartened and embittered, the burgher force broke up and rode for home.

Burgers, seeing his support melting away, compromised by building a row of forts along the border. He also raised a force of irregular soldiers, the Lydenburg Volunteers, from the local citizenry. To meet the costs of his abortive expedition and of the forts, he resorted to a 'war tax'. For the burghers, this was the last straw: to a man they refused to pay the tax.

The war came close to Pilgrim's Rest. The first brush with the Pedi took place on Henry Glynn's farm at Krugerspost, only a few kilometres away. It caused something approaching panic in the camp, and further enflamed resentment against the government, which the miners felt had left them to their fate. The transport services were discontinued; wagons in the Lydenburg area commandeered for active service; work on the diggings came to a standstill as a rough-and-ready defence system was organized. The women and children slept in a laager by night.

The diggers found a firebrand spokesman in Phelan, editor of the *Gold Fields Mercury*, an expanded version of his original broadsheet *Gold News*. In a virulent editorial, Phelan declared that those who were once for the government were now firmly against it; they could not serve a State which forced its laws upon its subjects, made them pay crippling taxes, yet failed to give them proper protection in times of danger.

According to a further edition of the newspaper, that of 28 August, 1876, the diggers even went so far as to hold a meeting to discuss the possibility of negotiating separate terms with Sekhukhune. They also resolved not to pay the war tax, and to tender their support for a plan inviting the British government to intercede between Sekhukhune and the Transvaal government. It was further suggested that the Republic should federate with the British colonies in southern Africa. Though nothing seems to have come of these manoeuvres, they do indicate the mood of the miners in this moment of deepening crisis.

Then, in November 1876, Phelan published a criticism of Dr John Scoble, MacDonald's successor as Gold Commissioner. Scoble felt the article brought him into contempt, had the journalist brought before him, fined him £27. 10s. and sentenced him to two weeks' imprisonment. The miners promptly held yet another meeting, marched to the gaol, reduced it to rubble with their picks, and released Phelan in defiance of the Commissioner and his policemen.

Scoble prudently retired to Lydenburg and, from there, a detachment of the Lydenburg Volunteers, 25-strong and armed with a cannon, was sent to deal with the diggers' 'mutiny'. The commando was led by the Irishman Aylward, who had no more faith in the government than had the miners. He left his men outside the camp and rode on alone to parley with the rebels. By this time, however, feelings had subsided, the diggers had gone back to work, and Phelan was back in his office scribbling more editorials. The upshot of Aylward's visit was yet another drunken orgy, in which the Irish captain was an enthusiastic participant. Eighteen of the ringleaders surrendered themselves voluntarily on a charge of disturbing the peace. They were released on bail, but never brought to trial.

Thus ended the Pilgrim's Rest 'rebellion' against the Transvaal government, which by now was approaching dissolution.

From Pilgrim's Rest as well as from Pretoria, surreptitious appeals were sent to Sir Henry Bulwer, Governor of Natal, and to Sir Henry Barkly, Governor of the Cape Colony, inviting the British to intervene. It wasn't long before they did so: in January 1877 Sir Theophilus Shepstone, with an escort of Natal police, rode into Pretoria. Three months later he announced the annexation of the Transvaal, declaring it a British colony. So demoralized and divided were the burghers that there was barely a protest as the Union Jack was raised and the official proclamation read out in the capital.

It was the end of President Burgers's career, and of his plans and visions for a great and independent new country. He left Pretoria, penniless and broken in spirit, never to return. His mission, after five well-meaning years, had failed.

Politics and progress

The diggers of Pilgrim's Rest, Mac Mac and Spitskop welcomed the new administration in their time-hallowed fashion – by getting gloriously drunk *en masse*. They were filled with the jingo spirit of Empire, and for a while Shepstone's popularity rode high, particularly when he remitted the special war tax and, in June 1877, disbanded the Lydenburg Volunteers.

But it soon enough became clear that annexation would not automatically resolve the muddle left behind by President Burgers. Shepstone had merely inherited the problems.

Among the most difficult of them was the recalcitrant Pedi king, Sekhukhune, who, having tried his luck against the Boers, now chanced it with the British. The Second Sekhukhune War was sparked by a series of attacks on farmers in the Lydenburg district. Early in November 1879, Sir Garnet Wolseley was sent to deal with the trouble. He had under his command 2 000 white soldiers and 8 000 Swazi auxiliaries. The two forces combined at the mouth of the Tjate Valley and then advanced on the main Pedi strongholds. On 23 November the hill fortress of Mkwame fell; two days later, after a token resistance, the hill Motswadibe – the 'Water Koppie' – was captured, providing an ideal position for the bombardment of Sekhukhune's capital. The British troops attacked before dawn, and by ten in the morning the king's stronghold was in flames. Sekhukhune retreated to caves in the 'Fighting Kop', and there followed a ferocious night battle to dislodge him. At the height of the assault, Sekhukhune himself managed to slip away and hole up in another cave, where he languished, half-starving, for three days before giving himself up. The caverns on the 'Fighting Kop' were blown up with gun-cotton, and the king, a thousand of his warriors dead on the battlefield, was locked up in Pretoria's gaol. From there he was later released, only to be murdered, shortly afterwards, by a rival for the throne.

The Lydenburg area had again been perilously close to the scene of violent action. The 94th Regiment, under Colonel R. P. Anstruther, was stationed in the town, and joined in the fighting at its height. After the close of hostilities, the regiment stayed on to protect the peace.

The next source of unrest was the miners themselves. They had reason for complaint.

The two wars against Sekhukhune had unnerved them; they felt the government should have provided surer protection. They wanted official assistance in prospecting and opening up new mining areas. Above all, they wanted an assurance that the long-promised railway line from Lydenburg to Lourenço Marques would actually materialize. The burghers had not managed to protect their interests; the British, they felt, could and surely would.

In the event, when Sir Theophilus eventually paid them a visit in 1879, they were sorely disappointed. He arrived at Pilgrim's Rest with several wagons and an escort of mounted troopers, to be met by a deputation of miners, who bluntly listed their needs. Shepstone, with equal bluntness, turned them all down. He had his hands full with the rest of the country, he said. There was no money, and in his private opinion the railway would never be built. The diggers, he intimated, would have to fend for themselves.

This was hardly what the miners were waiting to hear. So much for the great British government, come to rescue them! They had done better from old President Burgers. Before Shepstone departed, they vented their feelings in characteristic fashion. The Administrator had originally intended to bivouac for the night at Pilgrim's Rest, before moving on to Mac Mac and Spitskop. He quickly underwent a dramatic change of mind: the miners set fire to the grass around the camp, stampeding the troopers' horses, and drove away their oxen. At the same time they plied the escort with quantities of raw, fiery brandy. Finally, in unseemly and un-British haste, Shepstone and his party withdrew. Few of the escort were able to stay upright in the saddle, and most of them made their exit on their backs, strewn unconscious on the bottom of the wagons!

Behind all the miners' trouble lay one, basic, reality, which most of them were reluctantly coming to recognize: in the first two years of the boom at Pilgrim's Rest, over a million and a half pounds' worth of gold had been taken from the alluvial diggings, but the accessible reserves were rapidly being depleted. Many tons of gold-bearing ore still waited in the seams below the surface, but they were beyond the reach of the individual miner. British rule, no more than burgher rule, could not bring back the welcome glint of yellow metal in red earth. Inevitably the 'capitalists' began to gain over the 'free enterprise' men, many of whom now started to drift away in search of new fields. In the surrounding valleys, other finds were made, but none proved as rich as those of Pilgrim's Creek.

It was a disheartening time, made more so by a resumption of friction between Boer and Briton. For British rule in the Transvaal, established almost effortlessly, turned out to be a fragile thing, lasting little more than three years. During that time a new spirit entered the men of the Transvaal. The theft of their country had unified them, and they had found a strong natural leader in the doughty person of Paul Kruger, son of the Rustenburg hunter (see page 22). A series of appeals for the return of freedom fell on deaf ears, opposition intensified, gathering physical force in an outright rebellion. In December 1880 five thousand Republicans mobilized on the farm Paardekraal, near Krugersdorp, where a provisional government was elected under a triumvirate consisting of Kruger, ex-President Marthinus Pretorius and Pieter Joubert. On 15 December these men declared unilateral independence, and soon afterwards their government moved to new headquarters in Heidelberg. About 7 000 burghers obeyed the call to arms and were enrolled in three commandos.

War followed swiftly. The British attempted, without success, to reassert control; a series of abortive skirmishes left Boer unity unshaken. The hostilities culminated on 27 February 1881 in a disaster that shocked the government and people of Great Britain. Some 554 men under the command of General Sir George Colley took the field at Majuba, the 'Mountain of Doves', near Laing's Nek on the border between Natal and the Transvaal and, without supporting artillery, found themselves isolated on the crest, heavily outnumbered by the sharp-shooting Boers. In the débâcle that followed, Colley and 92 of his men were killed, 134 wounded. Among the Republicans, only one was killed and five wounded.

The Battle of Majuba brought to an end the First Boer War (or Transvaal War). President Brand of the Orange Free State helped to mediate the peace; Commandant-General Piet Joubert and Sir Evelyn Wood, Colley's successor, met near Laing's Nek on 6 March, 1881. They arranged a provisional armistice, which was followed by a full agreement. At the Pretoria Convention, on 8 August, self-government was returned to the Transvaal.

The war had its effect – as had the Sekhukhune tussle that preceded it – on life in the Lydenburg area. At the start of hostilities the 94th Regiment, under Colonel Anstruther, was still stationed at Lydenburg. The Colonel and most of his men were detached and sent to Pretoria, then under siege; the remaining 69 troops were left under the command of Second Lieutenant Long, who had orders to protect the British stores. With considerable ingenuity he improvised a system of defence. The camp consisted of a number of huts, some of which he pulled down for their bricks. He then built a series of walls to link eight of the huts in a rough square, a concoction of pulverised ant-heaps providing cement. Around the walls, the men dug a defence ditch, in which they planted land-mines. Beyond this was a thick thorn hedge, and a barrier of rubble to break the advance of horses. The thatched roofs of the huts were protected with sail cloth, and ammunition was concealed in an underground arsenal. Proud of his efforts, Long dubbed the place Fort Mary, in honour of his wife.

On 6 January 1881, Commandant Pieter Steyn entered Lydenburg without resistance. Thereafter, the Republicans held the town, but not the fort. Commandant-General Piet Joubert issued a surrender ultimatum, which was handed to Lieutenant Long, and which earned a forthright refusal.

There followed a protracted sniping and artillery exchange between fort and besiegers, two small Boer cannon duelling with an extraordinary British gun. This was constructed out of the barrel of an Abyssinian pump, so fashioned that it could lob a one-and-a-half-pound ball over the ramparts. A lot of damage was inflicted by the Boer guns, but Long was made of stern stuff. He quickly plugged the gaps in his defences, mending as much as he could, and went on fighting.

Early in March the Boers launched another and heavier attack on the battered Fort Mary, during which the thatched roofs were set alight. On 10 March an exasperated Joubert sent a further letter to the garrison demanding surrender. Long still refused to give up.

By now, however, news of the disaster at Majuba Hill had reached the town, and the start of peace negotiations rescued Long and his weary men from a third attack. For 85 days the garrison had withstood a siege by between two and three hundred Transvalers, during which time there had been only three British deaths. The fort itself survived for a few years more, until in 1889 the Boers used its bricks to build a powder magazine. This can still be seen, and bears inscriptions scratched on the brickwork by the British soldiers during the siege.

The miners of Pilgrim's Rest had barely recovered from this upheaval when their fortune took a further turn. Some mystery surrounds the man responsible for it, a London financier named David Benjamin.

Tradition has it that Benjamin opened his copy of the *Illustrated London News* one morning to find a description and pictures of the goldfields of the eastern Transvaal. The report must have had a powerful impact on him, for he was soon on his way to the Cape, from where he is believed to have travelled up to the goldfields on a tour of inspection. Not long afterwards, through a representative in Pretoria, he came to an arrangement with the Transvaal Volksraad.

In return for a substantial contribution to the country's coffers, Benjamin obtained a concession granting him mining rights over six farms in the Pilgrim's Rest area. The deed of concession was signed by Paul Kruger, Marthinus Pretorius, and W. Hollard, and Benjamin's signature was witnessed by the State Secretary, W. E. Bok, and the State Attorney, E. J. Jorissen. As recorded in the *Staats Courant*, the concession was 'granted and assured by the Government of the South African Republic to Mr David Benjamin of Cape Town in the Colony of the Cape of Good Hope on this, the 10th day of November, 1881, in consequence and by virtue of a Resolution passed by the Honourable Volksraad in its sittings of the 7th November, 1881. The Government of the South African Re-

public hereby grants and assures to the said David Benjamin, his successor or assignees, the full, free and exclusive right to all Gold Reefs and other mines, minerals, ores and precious stones of whatsoever nature now in, on or under the farms and lands named 'Ponieskrantz', 'Ledovine', 'Waterhoutboom', 'Grootfontein', 'Belvedere' and 'Driekop' (otherwise known as 'Pilgrim's Rest') situate in the district of Lydenburg in the South African Republic'.

In return for all this, Benjamin was to pay the government £1 000 a year and to guarantee that he would start his mining operations within a period of two years from the date of the concession. He was bound to employ 25 white miners and, in addition, had to compensate the diggers of Pilgrim's Rest and settle their claims.

Herein lay the rub. The diggers resolved to make this arch-'capitalist' pay as dearly as possible for their evictions. Complicated negotiations dragged on for the next two years, during which time Benjamin's agents paid out an unprecedented £70 000. One fortunate man received £12 000 in compensation, and many others received handsomely for claims they could no longer afford to mine themselves. Only after this flood-tide of litigation had abated was Benjamin in a position to begin his own operations – in 1883, when his Transvaal Gold Exploration Company was floated. Its Chairman was G. Maynard Farmer of Cape Town, though the majority of the shares were held in London. The local manager in the field was a young American mining engineer, Gardner Williams, who was later to attain prominence in Cecil Rhodes's empire.

With a gas engine and a mill installed at Pilgrim's Rest, the company was ready for full production. New, deeper levels of gold deposits were opened up, and the company's shareholders received increasingly larger dividends. By 1886 it was able to announce the recovery of £1 576-worth of gold. And this was only the start – the profit graph climbed spectacularly during the next decade, to reach a peak return of £69 000 in 1894.

The advent of Benjamin marked a major turning-point in the lives of the miners of Pilgrim's Rest. From now on the old, maverick way of life, the romantic amateurism of the early days, steadily succumbed to the new order. The individual digger was to survive for decades to come. Indeed, he was to last well into the present century. But his heyday was past. Capital, organization, heavy machinery capable of striking deep into the earth, geological know-how: these were the elements of the future. In the face of this challenge, many of the old-timers loaded up their belongings, took their compensation money, and tramped away in search of their ancient solitude. Others stayed, to become part of the new system. The change to a more settled way of life was reflected in a new style of architecture at Pilgrim's Rest, one which is still very much in evidence today.

Until now, the village, straggling along its winding creek and dusty road, had been a temporary affair, consisting mostly of tents and wattle-and-daub huts. Even its banks, canteens and church were hardly more durable than the dwellings. Though there was no provision for privately-owned land in the Benjamin holdings, there was need for a more permanent kind of home for the company's employees. The answer: prefabricated houses.

These had first been developed, in Britain in the early nineteenth century, by a London cabinet-maker named John Manning. They had been imported by the 1820 Settlers of the eastern Cape, and had proved particularly successful in areas lacking in natural wood. By mid-century designs had improved, wood and zinc comprising the basic structure. It was this type which was introduced to Pilgrim's Rest in the 1880s.

The houses came in the form of kits, with, according to the advertisements, 'everything complete, ready to put up at once'.

Pilgrims at rest. *Above left:* Chaitow's all-purpose shop in Edwardian days. *Centre left:* the horseless carriage was an established feature of the village by the 1920s, though its introduction to the rough tracks and deep valleys of the area had been cautious. The first to arrive was an aristocratic Hispano Suiza, prized possession of TGME's general manager; the second – inevitably – a Model-T Ford. *Below left:* Boer prisoners-of-war were interned in the region in late 1900. The Boers' 'Long Tom' Creusot field guns and knowledge of the rough terrain (*below*) enabled them to delay Sir Redvers Buller's advance from Lydenburg in the last months of the 'formal' phase of the Anglo-Boer War.

Plans, nails, screws, wood and zinc plates were all packed into a single unit, simple to transport, erect, and, if necessary, dismantle and move elsewhere. Some were imported, others manufactured in the country, though many of the parts and fittings for the latter had to be brought from overseas.

From the outside, the houses all looked more or less the same, but there was a certain variation in the internal arrangement of the rooms. The standard issue consisted of one large and two small rooms, a kitchen, and a verandah and, of course, floor and ceiling. There was also a steeply sloping roof, which was variously finished and decorated in the Victorian manner. Many of the houses on the steep sides of the valley were supported by poles to keep them level. Furniture was simple and sturdy, often knocked together out of old dynamite boxes; shelves decorated with cut-paper fringes; kitchen utensils of zinc or iron; the cooking done on imported wood-fired stoves.

The establishment of the Transvaal Gold Exploration Company coincided with an improvement in the economic fortunes of the South African Republic. In April 1883, after a number of years as a member of the ruling triumvirate, Paul Kruger was voted President by a clear majority. It was a significant choice. Over the next twenty years, in peace and war, Kruger's massive, brooding personality was to dominate the country, embodying the stubborn will of his people.

Conservative though he was, Kruger was nevertheless flexible enough to introduce shrewd economic innovations. The most significant of these was the sale of concessions, or monopolies, to 'Uitlander' investors. Benjamin's company had been one such concession but the first and most famous – or perhaps infamous – was the Hatherley Gin Distillery, the inspiration of the ubiquitous 'Count' Nellmapius.

With money earned from his mining enterprises, Nellmapius had bought the Hatherley farm, a few kilometres east of Pretoria, and began farming. Soon enough though, his nose for business led him in more profitable directions: in October 1881 he negotiated a concession from the government giving him sole rights to the refining of raw liquor from mealies, and for the refining of sugar. With a capital of £100 000 – a very handsome sum in those days – he formed a company, and in June 1882 began construction of a factory on the Hatherley property. This bizarre flower of the veld blossomed into a four-storey building, crammed with a bewildering array of pipes, tanks and machinery, with a large smoke-stack belching forth the reek of burning mealies. It was on this feature that, on 6 June, 1885, President Kruger broke a bottle of champagne when he officially declared the place open. He dubbed the project Volkshoop or 'People's Hope', but the people themselves called it Die Eerste Fabrieke – the historic 'First Manufactory' to appear in their young country. Soon the Hatherley Mill was busy poisoning the populace with its products.

While the gin factory flourished and brought much-needed revenue to the Transvaal, other and worthier national ambitions remained in abeyance. Among these was the long-awaited railway line linking the Republic with Delagoa Bay.

The alternative to a rail link was provided by the transport-riders, intrepid men who drove wagon-loads of supplies from Lourenço Marques to the Drakensberg escarpment and the diggers' encampments. Theirs was a tough, exhilarating life, spiced with a strong dash of danger. The road had hardly improved since the days of Louis Trichardt and his abortive trek, and they had to contend with wild animals, monsoon conditions in the rainy season, drought in summer, and the constant threat of malaria and yellow fever. The climax of the journey was the herculean struggle to get the wagons up the steep face of the 'Berg.

The last leg of the journey provided a stiff test for man and beast. The wagons were modified to cope with the climb, most being equipped with special rack brakes fitted to the back wheels,

which prevented the vehicles from rolling backwards, but even so the rear wheels often had to be tied with leather thongs. These held the wagon on the slope and saved the driver having to use his hand-brake, leaving him free to guide the oxen. Since the wagons could not lean more than a few inches to either side without risk of capsizing, they were forced to travel along the ridges and crests of the hills, which further complicated the route. Teams of twenty or more oxen were hitched to a wagon on the precarious ascent, which culminated in the long slope of Pilgrim's Hill.

At the end of all this, the transport-rider's profit was all-too-often discouragingly modest. The going rate for goods carried from Delagoa Bay to Pilgrim's Rest was about ten shillings per hundred pounds weight; the rate to Lydenburg was fifteen shillings. A wagon could hold around three tons of goods, so the transport-rider, if all went well, would earn about £15 on the Pilgrim's Rest run. But the journey took eight to ten days at best, and the vehicles suffered heavy wear and tear, to the point where they often had to be replaced at the end of a trip. When tsetse fly struck, a whole span of oxen might be wiped out. At a cost of about £8 per working ox, this was a loss the transport-rider could ill afford.

Little might be remembered of this curious breed of men if fortune had not set a poet in their midst.

In 1884 an eager young man named Percy FitzPatrick arrived on the goldfields. His first job was as a humble assistant storekeeper in Pilgrim's Rest. A glimpse of him at this moment of his life was left in the record of a visitor, J. B. Taylor, who visited the village store and found, behind an improvised counter, 'a typical rooinek, a youth of about twenty, red-haired, burnt, blistered and freckled by the sun, with eyes that tumbled with merriment and a smile that completely captivated me'.

But FitzPatrick soon tired of the mundane routine, and left to become, in succession, a prospector's hand and a journalist. He then bought himself a wagon, and went into business as a transport-rider.

He was on the road for about two years, from 1884 to 1886. The companion of his adventures was a bull-terrier of heroic tenacity, whom he called Jock. Many years later FitzPatrick was to entertain his four children with tales of Jock and his exploits. Set against a backcloth of creaking ox-wagons in the lonely wastes of the veld, these tales were to crystallize in one of the world's classic animal stories, *Jock of the Bushveld*. The saga of the runt of the litter who made good is closely modelled on the original, and the book has the charm of nostalgia for the days of youth and freedom. FitzPatrick vividly describes the atmosphere of the Lowveld, by turns exotic and menacing. Here is the reality of its swamps and rivers, its herds of game, its prowling lions, its many secret places, its sights, smells and sounds. Here are portrayed odd and eccentric characters – hunters, traders and explorers – withdrawn from civilization, living and working in a world of their own.

Among them was FitzPatrick's Zulu driver, the immortal Jim Makokel. A veteran of the battles of Isandlwana and Rorke's Drift in the Anglo-Zulu War in 1879, Jim remained a warrior to the core, reverting regularly to type. He formed an unholy alliance with Jock in their raids on the common enemy, the Shangaan mine-workers on their way to the diggings. Even the oxen are imbued with their own carefully delineated characters, exemplified in the powerful lead-oxen, struggling ever onwards as fever picks off the rest of the team.

But it is Jock who dominates the book. A passionate and resourceful hunter, he is also a brawler of the highest calibre. He follows FitzPatrick on every trail, doing battle with a wounded kudu bull, with a crocodile, and in one hair-raising scene besting a savage captive baboon at a wayside store. There is stirring action in this narrative, but also moments of tranquillity, especially at the end of the day. This was the hour of the camp-fire, of roasting meat, of the scents and sounds of the wild in the darkness beyond the light of the camp-fire.

For FitzPatrick, it was an experience never to be forgotten. But it was all too brief. On one disastrous trip fever caught up with him, and his spans of oxen were annihilated, leaving him penniless. He abandoned his wagons, passed Jock on to a friend, and surveyed new fields of adventure, of which a promising one was already at hand.

FitzPatrick's attention had been drawn to a new goldfield, centred on finds made in the Barberton area, in the great De Kaap Valley, on the edge of the escarpment to the south-east of the Lydenburg fields. Years before, Tom McLachlan had predicted that gold would one day be discovered in this wild and desolate valley. After the Benjamin take-over of Pilgrim's Rest, more and more prospectors drifted away to the south, and soon enough they came across the tell-tale traces of gold. At first the finds were scattered, but as time went on they became more localized.

The first major strike took place in a creek on the south-east side of the De Kaap Valley. There, on 3 June, 1883, August Robert, otherwise known as 'French Bob', discovered what came to be known as the Pioneer Reef. It was by far the single richest find yet made in Africa: an exposed quartz reef heavy with gold, up to half a metre in width on the surface and running for almost three kilometres. French Bob's monopoly on this treasure-trove did not last long. Within weeks a mass migration of miners threatened to swamp the valley. From his claim high on the hill, French Bob watched them bitterly. 'A carrion crow-like gathering', was how he later described them. 'They came to snatch the spoil from the hands of the toil-worn and ragged men who had hunted and brought down the prey.'

Other finds quickly followed, and soon a large area of the valley was pegged out. Then, in May 1885, a still bigger strike was made when the Yorkshireman Edwin Bray found his 'Golden Quarry', later to be named the Sheba Reef. It triggered a world-wide explosion of 'gold mania', in which overseas investors played a major part. The Sheba Reef Gold Mining Company was formed, with a capital of £15 000. The first 13 000 tons of ore milled realized 50 000 ounces of gold, and shares in the Sheba venture swiftly climbed to more than £100 apiece. Further companies were spawned at hectic speed, and the patchwork of claims became the subject of passionate debate on the world's stock exchanges, where investors argued the rival merits of the charmingly named New Chum and Twice Rejected, Nil Desperandum and Joe's Luck, Honeybird Creek and Lost Ten Tribes and many, many others. Altogether, a total of 108 separate companies were formed to work some four thousand claims on which payable gold had reputedly been found.

In contrast to the early diggings at Pilgrim's Rest, this was a hard, often brutal community. There were violent brawls, much robbery, frequent murder.

Hub of the fields were the stock exchanges which appeared almost overnight in the hitherto sleepy village of Barberton. There were two of them – the Kaap Exchange and the Transvaal Exchange – and they worked almost round the clock to handle the flood of scrip. Gold prices fluctuated wildly with the announcement of new discoveries or the 'pinching out' of established claims. Vast numbers of swindlers and speculators battened on this erratic market. Among the many beneficiaries of the Barberton field was David Benjamin. Viewed from London, his valley of Pilgrim's Creek and that of Barberton appeared more or less contiguous, and eager investors happily poured money into his company.

At the same time, taxes from the field helped to restore the economic health of the Republic, drained by its long series of crises. President Kruger paid a visit to the diggings, where he was warmly welcomed and made a speech, standing on a table, to the assembled diggers.

Watching all this, and becoming involved in it, was Percy Fitz-Patrick. Poverty-stricken after the collapse of his transport enterprise but as cheerful and alert as ever, he arrived in Barberton and went into partnership with a broker, Hirschel Cohen. They had interests in a number of properties, including a couple of hotels, and in the town's first newspaper, the *Barberton Herald*, which brought out its initial issue on 4 May, 1886. FitzPatrick wrote a racy column, 'Chat of the Camp'. The partners also acted as stock-jobbers, and held shares in a number of mining ventures, including one discovered by FitzPatrick himself – the Revolver Mine. In fact there was hardly a gold-plated pie in which they did not have a finger or two.

FitzPatrick expressed the view – in the *Herald* – that the Barberton field had a long and glorious future ahead of it. It was an opinion he held right up until the bubble burst, early in 1887.

Over-speculation in under-developed mines, over-capitalization of the working properties and large-scale swindling all combined to hasten the crash. Outlying villages such as Eureka City were the first to go, leaving only scattered ruins to attract the curiosity of posterity. Much of the old business centre of Barberton was gutted by fire in January 1891, a conflagration from which even the Phoenix Hotel failed to rise. Almost overnight, the boom town became a ghost town. Hundreds of investors had been misled, and they lost heavily, though when the dust had settled there were still many workable claims in operation which continued to pay dividends to those lucky enough to have a stake in them.

From the first fossickings in the eastern Transvaal by men such as Marais and Mauch, through to the strikes at Spitskop, Mac Mac and Pilgrim's Rest, and finally to the rich deposits of the Barberton field, had run a golden thread of discovery, each new find overshadowing the one before. By now, too, a legal and administrative apparatus had brought orderliness to the goldfields. A new technology was developing the machinery for retrieving the gold, even from deeply-sited reefs and deposits.

Given all these conditions, the next discovery seemed like the happiest of Fate's fingers. In March 1886, in an area crossed by many thousands of luckless prospectors in the past decades, gold reef was discovered. The area was the Witwatersrand, the 'Ridge of White Waters', and the first finds were made by two men, the Australian George Harrison and a Lancashire coal-miner named George Walker.

On the surface, the reef stretched for some thirty kilometres. Its depth, however, could only by guessed at. There was nothing to tell the prospectors that they had stumbled on the greatest goldfield on earth, and that eldorado was at hand.

The glittering prize

The surface deposits on the Witwatersrand were merely the hors d'oeuvres to a vast banquet of gold.

It would be many years before the Reef's full extent was revealed. Today's estimate of the overall quantities is some hundred times as great as the most optimistic guess at the turn of the century. In comparison with the 20 million tons of ore mined in the Lydenburg fields, a monumental 6 000 million tons has so far been brought up from the deep deposits on the Rand.

Almost immediately, a raw and raffish settlement began to sprawl over the bleak and wind-scoured Highveld ridge. Laid out on the government farm 'Randjeslaagte', not far from the diggings, the new town was surveyed and named Johannesburg early in November 1886. It grew rapidly, playing genial and undemanding host to the now-familiar regiments of diggers, accompanied by a crowd of speculators, bankers and saloon-keepers and an unhealthy sprinkling of the world's criminal elements. From this human flux, a commercial infrastructure quickly emerged: by the end of 1897 there were 67 companies operating in the area. By then, too, the more than one thousand stamps had refined some 23 000 ounces of gold. Less than a decade later there were 200 companies, controlled by ten major finance houses, predominant of which was that of Wernher, Beit & Co.

The company's original base had been in the diamond fields of Kimberley, where the activities of Julius Wernher and Alfred Beit had been backed by the resources of Jules Porges et Cie, the great Paris diamond merchants. Wernher controlled the London end of the company's operations, while Beit remained in South Africa. When Beit received samples of gold from the Witwatersrand, he quickly turned his attention to exploiting the new treasure-house. As his representative in the goldfields he chose Hermann Eckstein, assisted by J. B. Taylor. Their adviser in mining matters was Lionel Phillips, a veteran of fifteen dusty years in Kimberley. The firm of H. Eckstein & Co, soon to become popularly known as The Corner House, was incorporated in 1889 as Wernher, Beit's major subsidiary.

When Hermann Eckstein died in Stuttgart in January 1893, his place at the head of the firm was taken by the diminutive but energetic Lionel Phillips. It was he who was responsible not only for guiding the company's fortunes on the Rand, but also for directing its attention towards the potential in the Lydenburg fields.

In the first few years of its life the Witwatersrand had far outstripped its historic predecessor, but Phillips believed that the capital and technology which had opened up the Rand could well bring new life to the eastern Transvaal. That the potential existed had already been proved by the performance of Benjamin's Transvaal Gold Exploration Company, which had made rapid strides, opening up a complex of mines eccentrically named after letters of the ancient Greek alphabet, though who precisely was responsible for this display of classical erudition remains a mystery. Among the mines on Ponieskrantz were the Alpha, Beta, Eta, Theta, Iota, Kappa, Chi and Nu. Of these, two were to become particularly famous: the Theta, opened in December 1888, turned out to be the richest in the district. It was closely followed by the Beta, which was still producing gold 75 years after its discovery. The combined revenues from these mines, in 1894, totalled £69 000. Thus it was hardly surprising that the magnates of the Rand turned some of their attention to Pilgrim's Rest.

There is no record of the date on which Lionel Phillips initiated negotiations with Benjamin. The outcome of their discussions, though, is well attested: Eckstein's and Transvaal Gold Exploration were amalgamated to form a new and larger company, incorporated at first as Beit and Phillips but soon renamed the Lydenburg Gold Mining Estates Ltd, and renamed yet again the following year to become the Transvaal Gold Mining Estates Limited (or TGME), under which title it would continue to operate until the last mine closed down in 1971.

The first board meeting of the new company was held at The Corner House headquarters in Johannesburg on 20 May, 1895. Phillips took the chair. With him around the table were his directors, most of whom had a working knowledge of the Drakensberg goldfields. They included Percy FitzPatrick and Abe Bailey. The buoyant FitzPatrick, now 33, had come a long way in a few years since he had abandoned his transport wagon, while the irrepressible Bailey, having amassed a fortune from his New Clewer Estate in Barberton, was already, at 30 years of age, an old hand in the goldfields. FitzPatrick's old partner, Hirschel Cohen, had been appointed Company Secretary: having fallen on hard times since the bursting of the Barberton bubble, he was now happy enough to work for £30 a month.

In the weeks following that first meeting Lionel Phillips went on a full-scale buying spree through the Lydenburg area – combining business with a great deal of pleasure. After his years in the near-desert of Kimberley, he was entranced by the beauty of the mountains. It was to be the first of many visits.

Phillips had a sure 'nose for gold', but he always backed intuition with careful investigation. He systematically bought all the properties where payable gold had been found but where the miners had been unable to strike deep through lack of funds and machinery. Besides the workings at Pilgrim's Rest, the company soon owned some 200 000 acres sprawling across an area fifty kilometres long, with mineral rights over a further 70 000 acres. Thus, by the end of 1895, everything seemed set for fortune.

But then, suddenly, disaster struck. It took the form of the Jameson Raid, in which the directorate of TGME was deeply implicated.

In the years since Majuba Hill tension had mounted between the leaders of the South African Republic in Pretoria and the 'Uitlanders' of the Witwatersrand.

Until the discovery of the Rand goldfields, relations between the mining population and the Boers had, on the whole, been amicable enough. The new fields had generated greatly increased revenues for the Republic, but the wealth brought its own problems. Whereas the Lydenburg fields were almost on the country's borders, those of the Rand were uncomfortably close – within a day's ride, in fact – of the capital. What had hitherto been little more than vague unease in the burghers' minds now became rapidly deepening suspicion. For while the old-style prospector had little interest in anything beyond the boundaries of his claim and the cost of living, the magnates of the Rand, the 'gold-bugs', had a passionate preoccupation with political as well as financial power. This became an open issue with their demand for 'Uitlander rights' – for the vote.

In this they came up against the stubborn spirit of Paul Kruger, who knew only too well that to enfranchise the Uitlanders, by now more numerous than the Boers of the Republic, would effectively hand the country over to them.

Their demands repeatedly thwarted, the Johannesburgers, led by the mine owners, hatched a plot to take over the Republic by force. Masterminding the conspiracy was the 'Reform Committee', of which Phillips was the chairman. Cecil Rhodes, head of Consolidated Diamonds and Prime Minister of the self-governing Cape Colony, was also deeply involved in the scheme. The plan was worked out in detail by Phillips, Rhodes, Rhodes's brother Frank, John Hays Hammond, and Dr Leander Starr Jameson. Fitz-Patrick and Abe Bailey also lent their enthusiastic support.

In contrast to the professionalism of their business methods, the organization of the rebellion was an amateur affair. Code-named the 'Flotation', it was to begin with an uprising in Johannesburg timed to coincide with the arrival of an expeditionary force led by Jameson – 'Doctor Jim' – from the Bechuanaland border. There, at Pitsani, he assembled something over 500 Rhodesian mounted police drawn from Cecil Rhodes's Chartered Company. At the last moment, however, Rhodes sensed impending failure and called off the rising in Johannesburg. At the same time, he sent an urgent telegram to Jameson instructing him to stay his hand. But by then Jameson had cut the telegraph wires, and the message failed to reach him. On 29 December, 1895 he led his men across the border and made for the Rand.

By 2 January the raiders had reached Doornkop, within a few hours' ride of Johannesburg, where they were surrounded by government troops. There followed a brief, violent skirmish in which seventeen of Jameson's miniature army were killed and 55 wounded. The remainder surrendered, and were ignominiously marched off to gaol in Pretoria, to be joined shortly afterwards by the leaders of the Reform Committee, including Phillips, Frank Rhodes, Bailey, FitzPatrick and John Hays Hammond.

While Jameson was deported to England for trial, the others were charged with high treason, and four of them, including Lionel Phillips, sentenced to death. The knowledge that their Chairman was sitting in Pretoria gaol listening to the sound of the gallows being hammered together outside his cell window did little to reassure TGME's London shareholders, who were in a highly nervous state. The first Annual General Meeting, of course, had to be postponed, but even in the shadow of the gallows Phillips's commercial zeal remained unimpaired, and he continued to conduct a brisk business from the gaol compound.

Then, on 11 July, 1896, President Kruger commuted the capital sentences to a fine of £25 000 each. The conspirators also had to give an undertaking not to meddle again in the political affairs of the Transvaal, either directly or indirectly. Kruger handed over the culprits to an embarrassed British government, fully aware of the psychological advantages flowing from so generous a gesture. An enquiry was held at the Cape, and Cecil Rhodes resigned as Prime Minister of the Colony. Another was conducted in London in 1897, after which Jameson and his officers – by now enjoying the status of popular heroes – received nominal sentences.

Even before all this dust had settled, the mines were again at full production. But they operated against a background of intensifying mistrust.

Phillips resigned his chairmanship of TGME, but remained the company's guiding spirit. Meanwhile, development of the fields at Pilgrim's Rest went on apace, an overhaul of ore crushing and transportation methods being the most significant development.

When the merger with Benjamin's company had taken place, most of the mines were still either open-cast workings or adits on the hillsides. These were serviced by a number of mills, powered by a small hydro-electric plant on the banks of the Blyde River at the foot of Brown's Hill, a system vulnerable to the vagaries of the river's flow: in summer there was normally enough water to keep the mill running, but in the dry months of winter, when the flow tended to dwindle to a near-trickle, the station often came to a standstill.

Changes to this frustrating state of affairs came with the ap-

pointment of TGME's first consulting engineer at Pilgrim's Rest, a man named Wertheman. He cast a critical eye over the distribution of the various workings from which ore was being recovered, and immediately decided that there should be a large central mill serving all the operating mines as well as those planned for the future. Of the existing mills, he scrapped all but two: the old mill built by Benjamin at Pilgrim's Rest, and a 20-stamp mill at Kameel's Creek, nestled in a picturesque setting among the hills to the west. He advised the company to construct a central, modern 60-stamp battery at Pilgrim's Rest, where the ore from the producing mines could be treated in a single process. Centralization, however, meant that the ore had to be carried longer distances, so Wertheman designed a special railway system connecting the main mill, through a series of branch lines, with the mines. Each line ended in a terminus, from where rows of cocopans were carried up the mountain sides to the various adits and, filled with ore, brought down again to be tipped into the waiting trucks and then drawn by electric tram to the main mill. Construction of the twelve kilometres of track involved was completed in 1897.

With the building of the new mill and the railway system came a need for a greater supply of electric power. Wertheman solved the problem by enlarging the existing power-station on the Blyde River and building a water-race from higher up the river. Two metres wide and a metre and a half deep, the race ran four kilometres to Brown's Hill. The power-station could now keep going in almost all weathers, supplying ample year-round current for the mill and the railway.

The Transvaal Gold Mining Estate's investment in the eastern Transvaal began to pay off, its profits from Pilgrim's Rest adding significantly to those from its Witwatersrand holdings.

A great deal of money, in fact, was being generated on the Rand. But the expansion of the gold-mining industry, far from ensuring a prosperous peace, actually brought the country closer to war. In the last half-decade of the century the Republican government, at increasingly bitter odds with the Uitlanders, used the revenue from the mines to finance the purchase of arms from Europe. These included two important items: the new German Mauser smokeless rifle and the French-built Creusot siege-gun. The latter, soon to be immortalized as 'Long Tom', was a formidable weapon, weighing several tons and capable of hurling a 38 kilogram shell a distance of ten kilometres.

In 1897 the progress towards open conflict was given impetus by the arrival of a new British High Commissioner at the Cape – Sir Alfred Milner. During the next three years, in collaboration with British Colonial Secretary Joseph Chamberlain, Milner set out to precipitate a war between Britain and the Transvaal. Using the Uitlander vote as the central issue, he manoeuvred and shifted his ground in so cynically skilful a manner that Kruger's diplomatic overtures repeatedly broke down – a tortuous and, for the Boers, a depressingly frustrating process that finally came to a head at the Bloemfontein Conference of June 1899. After the collapse of these negotiations, the pace accelerated towards a 'continuation of politics by other means'. The South African Republic sought common cause with President Brand's Orange Free State. The British landed troops in Durban; early in October 1899 the Boer leaders sent an ultimatum to the British. Its expiration on 11 October signalled the outbreak of the Second Anglo-Boer War.

It was both a new war, and an old one. Its roots lay far back, in the British invasion of the Cape at the end of the eighteenth century, in the emancipation of the slaves, in the Great Trek, in Shepstone's annexation of the Transvaal, in Majuba Hill. But at its heart lay the new gold, the prize upon which the Empire-builders had set their minds. And it seemed an easy prize, to be had for the taking. In London, it was confidently predicted that the war would be over by Christmas.

But the Anglo-Boer War was to drag on for more than two years – the twentieth century's first major international conflict.

In the first six months, the British were both over-confident and under-manned. They underestimated their opponent: the Boers, far from being the rag-tag rabble of rural amateurs that the British expected, were well armed, well organized and determined. They also had an intimate knowledge of the terrain and, in men such as Louis Botha, Christiaan de Wet and Koos de la Rey, military leaders capable of using the lie of the land to brilliant advantage.

The British opened two fronts, one in Natal under Commander-in-Chief General Sir Redvers Buller, the other under General Lord Methuen along the northern borders of the Cape Colony. On both fronts they came up against the Boer forces in entrenched positions, from which the smokeless Mauser repeater rifles could be used to devastating effect. The result was a series of set-piece battles in which the British suffered costly and humiliating defeats, and which reached its climax on 24 January, 1900 with the massacre on Spionkop.

Gradually, however, the tide turned in favour of the British. Lord Roberts replaced Buller as Commander-in-Chief and, with his Chief of Staff Kitchener, arrived on the massively reinforced western front. In Natal Buller finally crossed the Tugela to relieve besieged Ladysmith, and the two armies moved northwards to converge on the Transvaal. The final and longest-lasting phase of the war featured a protracted and increasingly bitter guerilla campaign waged by the Boers. The British answer to this defiance was a programme of wholesale farm-burning and the internment, in concentration camps, of many thousands of Boer women and children and of countless numbers of rural blacks.

Mining operations on the Rand and in the eastern Transvaal closed down during the war. On the eve of the conflict, all The Corner House companies moved to Cape Town, taking with them their minute books and ledgers. Consequently, once the republican authorities had taken over the mines, there was virtually no further communication between the caretakers left behind on the TGME's properties and the new head office, nearly 2 000 kilometres away.

During the closing stages of the conflict, the Boer forces in the field ran critically short of ready cash. Roving commandos, such as that of Jan Smuts, subsisted largely upon what provisions they were able to wring from the local tribespeople, who showed a notable reluctance to co-operate. Initially the only form of payment the Boers could offer was Republican bank-notes – by now almost worthless – but in due course gold coinage made its magical appearance, instantly conjuring up the necessary supplies of meat and mealies.

In June 1900, as Lord Roberts's 'Grand Army' moved ponderously up to swallow first the Free State towns and then those of the Transvaal, General Smuts appropriated the bar gold from the recently established Pretoria Mint and from the banks in Johannesburg. More of the metal was collected around Lydenburg, where General Ben Viljoen was in command. Viljoen sent his men to the reduction works in the Pilgrim's Rest area to scrape all the plates and carry off the amalgam. Thus a substantial hoard was accumulated. But gold in the form in which it was acquired couldn't be used to buy supplies in the field. What was needed was a source of readily usable coins of the realm, of accredited value. From this came the idea of establishing a small experimental mint.

By now the Witwatersrand was occupied by the British, so the obvious site for the mint was Pilgrim's Rest. Here there was little danger of a surprise attack from the British, for the valley formed a natural fortress. And the TGME workshop contained all the tools and equipment which might be needed.

A wagon carried the gold to the village, where it was stored under guard in the mine office, and a Mint Commission was appointed with all due formality. Its first act was to send an urgent message to the Boer government in the field asking for official permission to mint sovereigns. Once this had been obtained, the *Staatsmunt te Velde* – the 'State Mint in the Field' – and the *Staatsdrukkery te Velde* – the 'State Printing Press in the Field' – were established. The former headmaster of a school in Barberton, P. J. Kloppers, was appointed Head of the Mint and given a small group of assistants.

Kloppers' first plan was to bypass the minting of conventional coins altogether. His scheme was to refine the gold, roll it, then cut it up into squares. These would weigh slightly more than the official Kruger sovereigns, and could be used to buy the standard coins from those of the population who had hoarded them. The Mint Commission, however, rejected this notion. If he was to mint coins, they told him, they must look like coins.

Kloppers and his small team set to work. Their equipment, comprising a set of hammers and dies and a home-made press, was simple but effective. Over the following months, they produced a total of 986 *veld ponde*, each stamped with the legend *Een Pond 1902*. Slightly thicker than the Kruger sovereign, they contained, at the time of minting, gold of an average value of 22 shillings. Their nominal worth, however, is only a fraction of their present value, for the 'veld ponde' are now ranked among the world's rarest and most prized coins.

Together with the Mint went the State Printing Press in the Field, which was responsible for the production of paper money. It made use of the press at Pilgrim's Rest, probably the one used by Phelan to print his *Gold Fields Mercury*. Kloppers made a copper plate of the Republican coat-of-arms, and manufactured his own brand of printing ink. For paper he used pages cut from the TGME ledgers and old school exercise books. From these basic materials he printed notes with denominations of £1, £5 and £10.

Notwithstanding the benefit of a viable currency, the slow momentum of defeat continued.

After the relief of Ladysmith, Buller's army crossed the border into the Transvaal and rolled north in pursuit of Louis Botha's forces. On 7 September, 1900 the British captured Lydenburg after only token resistance. But there was a sting in the tail, for the Boer forces withdrew to the heights overlooking the town from the east, up the road now known as the Long Tom Pass. Besides the Creusot siege-gun which was to give its name to the pass, they had several other, smaller, artillery pieces. As the 'Tommies' bedded down in Lydenburg, the voice of the Long Tom boomed down at them from the edge of the mountain.

Next day the British forces moved out of Lydenburg and advanced up the long, winding pass to deal with this annoying piece of rearguard resistance, but, as so often happens in war, the mopping up operation turned out to be tougher in practice than it had seemed in theory. It was only with difficulty that the Boers were dislodged from a series of cleverly chosen defensive positions, their retreat farther up the pass being covered by artillery. Eventually, a clammy mist obscured the heights and fighting abated for the night. Buller returned to the offensive the following morning, and succeeded in driving the Boers to the edge of the escarpment and down the steep slope overlooking the great vista of the Lowveld.

Perched on a precarious incline, Long Tom continued to lob its heavy shells up at the British who, from their vantage point, could see the wagons of the Boer supply-convoy drawing slowly away over the 'Devil's Knuckles', a particularly hair-raising stretch of the

the road. The cavalry were sent in pursuit, but were soon driven back by the terrain and by the big gun.

The action continued relentlessly all day. By nightfall, the British had brought up their own artillery, and, at dawn on 10 September, set about a determined shelling of the Boer position. The Gordon Highlanders, meanwhile, were given the task of clearing the road over the Devil's Knuckles. It was only at four in the afternoon that the Boers withdrew from their positions in the Knuckles, sending thirteen of their wagons crashing over the nearby precipice to prevent their capture. As the sun set, the main Boer force, still in possession of the Long Tom, melted away into the gathering darkness.

By the end of 1901, lack of resources coupled with physical exhaustion had caught up with the now heavily outnumbered Boers. Louis Botha began peace initiatives, though the men of the Free State continued to fight.

On the Witwatersrand, and at Pilgrim's Rest, the mines were put under protection until such time as they could be handed over to the British. On 31 May, 1902, the Boer leaders met at Vereeniging before signing the peace treaty at Melrose House, Pretoria.

During the next eight years the republics of the Transvaal and Orange Free State and the two colonies of Natal and the Cape of Good Hope would, through statesmanship and a willingness to forgive the past, be forged together into a single country. This was the era of Union.

But the immediate post-war years were bleak. Thousands of people needed to be resettled. The land was devastated, and recovered with agonizing slowness. The mines of the Rand, though, were soon back in production.

The Lydenburg fields took longer to reach their pre-war output; 1908 saw a last, brief, gold-rush in the old style at Graskop, not far from the Jubilee Mine; and, as always, nature made her own special contributions to the story of the times, the most spectacular being the storm that broke over the Transvaal on 20 January, 1909 – the greatest in the country's recorded history.

For days beforehand the clouds built up from one end of the country to the other. The rain began to fall on the evening of the 20th, and within a very short time developed into a nation-wide cloudburst which lasted, without ceasing, for seven hours. Then, after a brief intermission, it began all over again, continuing for another eight hours. The rain gauges registered their maximum reading of eight and a half inches (226 millimetres) before running over. Indeed, it was estimated that fully 20 inches (508 millimetres) of rain fell in the course of the night. At the height of the downpour, the few brave souls who ventured out found it almost impossible to breathe in the engulfing sheet of water. Widespread and catastrophic flooding followed, reaching a tragic scale on the Witwatersrand. Over 150 men were trapped in the deep mine shafts; only 23 of them, miraculously preserved in a mine-shaft above the flood, were saved.

At Pilgrim's Rest the deluge struck with awesome force. The area's oldest inhabitant later reported to the *Star* newspaper that it was the worst in his memory. Thousands of tons of rock were washed loose to roll down Jubilee Hill. Great chunks were torn from the banks of the Blyde River, which rose ten metres, its roaring torrent cutting the village off from the outside world. All the bridges across the river were swept away, including the stone Joubert Bridge, built in 1896 and named after the Mining Commissioner. Though the main TGME mill survived intact, the power-station at the Jubilee Mine vanished altogether, and long stretches of the electric tramway were uprooted.

The flood cost the company £32 000 in loss of profit during the three months needed for repairs and rebuilding. The mill was closed until damaged adits were cleared and made safe. A further £12 400 of 'extraordinary expenditure' was incurred in the rebuilding of the bridges and in relaying the tram-track. As a result, the annual dividend was reduced to 7,5 per cent.

The next few years, though, saw a remarkable return to prosperity, yielding a bonanza for the investors. By the time of the Act of Union in 1910, the mines of the eastern Transvaal were employing some 250 whites and about 3 000 blacks. In that year, too, there was a major advance with the construction of the Belvedere power-station, sited near the junction of the Blyde and Treur rivers and formally opened the following year by General Smuts. The boom lasted from 1910 to 1915, during which time TGME ploughed about £100 000 a year into new development and the exploration of new seams. Over 500 000 ounces of gold were produced, earning a net profit of £1 912 000. The record year was 1914, with a net profit of £285 486. Much of this affluence was created by the Theta Mine, which had reached the zenith of its productivity. Its 'jeweller's boxes', heavy with visible gold, assayed up to 50 ounces to the ton. Indeed the ore was so rich and could so easily be extracted that iron gates, locked at the end of each day's work, were installed at the entrance to the mine.

But if company men and investors were gratified, for the individual miner these were the ember-years. Two men's stories typify the fate of the old-style digger. In about 1913 Tucker and McLanigan went into partnership to work a claim on Ledouphine, north-east of Pilgrim's Rest. They hit upon a rich leader which, within a short space of time, had brought them some £63 000. This was wealth beyond all their dreams, but they were single-minded in their expenditure, investing their gains almost exclusively in kegs of whisky. After a brief spell in Botha's Natal Horse during the First World War, they returned to their claim, to their jars of nuggets and barrels of hard tack. But then, one day, Nature took back what had so generously been given. The leader 'pinched out', and what had seemed an unending flow of gold ceased overnight. Tucker and McLanigan found themselves staring at an empty wall of rock. Unable to face the prospect of life without gold or whisky, they both committed suicide by taking cyanide.

With this defiant gesture, Tucker and McLanigan turned away from the future and, with many hundreds of others of their kind, slipped quietly into the past.

Overleaf: Kearney's Creek crevice, near Trout Pools, Mount Sheba. Kearney was one of the more successful of the area's original miners. The deep ravine named after him, in shadow for much of the time, supports dense sub-tropical plant life.

Planting for prosperity

From the turn of the century, the tenor of life in the eastern Transvaal began to change. The landscape took on a new look. The mines, after many decades of active and profitable life, slowly began to be phased out – despite the introduction of high-powered modern mining technology. Great man-made forests were introduced to the area, permanently altering its character. With the closure of the last mines in the early 1970s, a new if more modest industry, tourism, developed around the village of Pilgrim's Rest.

The first signs of these changes appeared with the area's slow emergence from isolation. In the years after the Anglo-Boer War new communications and transport, including the telegraph, the railway and finally the motor-car, in the popular phrase of the time, 'annihilated distance'. The first telegraph line marched across the hills from Lydenburg to Pilgrim's Rest in 1903. The following year it was extended to Krugerspost and Sabie, and by 1909 the complex covered the whole escarpment region. The police station in Pilgrim's Rest was allocated the area's first telephone number – Number Three – which it still retains. And a year later the mining company also received its own line to the outside world.

If the telegraph was a relatively recent novelty, the debate over the railway was by now of long standing. Innumerable proposals had been put forward in past decades for a line linking Lydenburg with Lourenço Marques. The transport of ore and supplies posed a major problem for the mine management, and a costly one at that. Repeatedly, the company's board had asked that a line be built to Pilgrim's Rest to relieve the pressure.

In principle, this was a sound idea. It was opposed, however, in a number of quarters. The Department of Mines objected to the concession granting TGME rights over a large area of land. The building of a railway, the government representatives felt, would simply be using public money to increase the profits of a private company. The directors of TGME parried each of these reservations during a series of meetings in 1909. They had little trouble in establishing the legitimacy of their concession, which had been renewed by the Milner government after the war. They also argued that their activities provided the area's economic lifeblood. Far from exploiting the railway, they would use it to encourage investment in the region as a whole. As an earnest of their intention, they offered to pay for any losses incurred by the railway, and to guarantee interest at three per cent on the cost of the building, to a limit of £400 000. They would also rent the section of the line which ran through their property.

Faced with these generous proposals, the government representatives agreed to the project. The money was voted – after what had by then been a generation's delay – and work began in 1910. The first stretch to be laid down ran from Nelspruit to Sabie, from where it was taken northwards to the terminus on the rim of the 'Berg at Graskop. The company's freight still had a 12-kilometre haul across the valley and over the mountains to Pilgrim's Rest, but this was a great advance on what had previously been a situation of almost total isolation. The line was completed and officially opened, with much speechmaking and flourish, in 1914. The whole population of the area turned out to welcome the first train as it chugged into Graskop station. It was a complete success, not only for its ability to transport goods, but also for enabling the populace easy and much-enjoyed access to the world beyond. A trip which once took weeks by ox-wagon, to Nelspruit or across the Lowveld to Lourenço Marques, for example, could now be comfortably fitted into a Sunday afternoon.

The railway, catering for the mass public, had an immediate and powerful impact. The new internal combustion engine began, however, as something of an object of curiosity, an elitist fad. Its introduction to the steep valleys around Pilgrim's Rest was extremely cautious. Such roads as did exist were rough tracks, rutted by generations of wagon-wheels and battered by the floods of rainy seasons. And if the downhill stretch on Pilgrim's Hill had its perils, the journey back up again was even more critical, for should the car not be able to make the gradient, it was doomed either to spend the rest of its life in the valley or to be ignominiously dragged out by a team of oxen. Indeed, in years to come, prospective car-buyers were to use the hill as a test of their intended purchase. If the car managed the hill, the salesman clinched the deal.

The two earliest vehicles to brave their way in and out of Pilgrim's Rest, however, did so with a flourish. The first to arrive was an aristocrat, an Hispano Suiza, pride and joy of the dapper Stephano Aimetti, TGME's general manager of the time. Next to make its appearance was the ubiquitous Model-T Ford, the first mass-produced popular car. The records show that it rose creditably to the challenge, making just four stops to cool off on the way back up the hill. Perhaps it also employed some of the other, ingenious tactics evolved by early motorists on the local roads. On steeper slopes, for example, it was advisable to go up backwards. There were two good reasons for this: then, as now, reverse gear was more powerful than the forward gears, and, secondly, the fuel system imposed certain limitations. In vintage cars, the petrol tank was located under the front seat, from where gravity alone led the petrol through to the carburettor. On a steep slope facing forwards, the supply of petrol would be cut off, so the simple answer was to travel in reverse!

Thus, within a few short years, new links were forged between the mining area and the outside world. Yet almost at the moment when the transport situation was resolved, the first small signs of mining decline became apparent. The phasing-out process was slow, stretching out across half a century, and marked by as many twists and turns as a country road in the 'Berg. The years before the First World War, when Aimetti was manager, were the last great boom period, reaching its peak with the record earnings of 1914. At the outbreak of the war Aimetti returned to Italy, to be succeeded as general manager, in 1915, by Richard Barry.

It was Barry's melancholy fortune to face the first of the company's serious setbacks, prelude to which was widespread flooding, the consequence of almost 70 inches (1 778 millimetres) of rain, in the year of his arrival. There were, too, the effects of more distant events, including the thunderous guns of the European war, half a world away. Costs rose steeply, reaching 18 shillings per ton of ore mined, and profits plummeted. From £219 000 in 1915, they fell to £167 000 in 1916, £138 000 in 1917, and to £93 000 in 1918. But all this was just the slope before the precipice – the dizzying plunge of earnings in 1919 to an all-time low of £15 000. The dividend that year was a miserable and unprecedented 2,5 per cent.

It was a bleak graph. And had the low prevailed, it might have brought a premature end to the company's operations. But the flight from gold later in the year fortuitously reversed the trend. The mines earned a healthy premium on their production, and profits rose to £89 000. They remained at that level for another two years before a further slump came in 1922, reducing them to £28 000.

This time the downward spiral continued. In 1923, despite an output of over 60 000 ounces of gold, the company showed a loss. Revenue from a number of other sources gave a nominal profit of £1 597, but this was scant consolation either to the directors or to the increasingly alarmed and critical shareholders.

Most of the latter were in London, and few had first-hand experience of the problems facing their company in the eastern Transvaal. Apart from the vagaries of the country's post-war economy, there were technical difficulties, in nearly every one of the thirteen deep mines which now produced the bulk of the ore – problems caused by underground water, 'water bodies' and devastating 'mud rushes'. At special risk were two of the mines – Elandsdrift and Vaalhoek – where great quantities of water accumulated in rifts in the dolomite. Even with the installation of expensive pumping equipment, disaster was never very far away. In 1927, for example, blasting in the Elandsdrift mine opened a fissure and a 'great, uncontrollable body of water' poured into the workings. In November 1928 the Vaalhoek mine, whose eighteen years of operation had been plagued by recurrent flooding, had to be shut down. Not only was the closure a blow to the company, but it was superstitiously regarded by the mining population as an omen.

Aside from all this, though, there remained a single, undeniable reason for loss of revenue. The gold was running out.

The region had come a long way since the days of Wheelbarrow Alec and his solitary discovery of September 1873. In those early days, the alluvial gold had lain in abundance close to the surface. Nature's generosity was to be had for the price of an aching back. Besides rich deposits of fine gold, there had been many nuggets of almost pure metal. But by the end of the first decade, the bulk of this easy wealth had been cleaned out, and miners had to dig deeper. The task demanded corporate endeavour, an approach first adopted by David Benjamin and then by TGME. Initially they had concentrated on extracting the main quartz leaders close to the surface, a type of gold easily recovered and one, moreover, which contained many of the famed 'jeweller's boxes'. Other ores near the surface were of the decomposed or oxidised kinds, also easily handled in the cyanide process.

But as the upper levels were exhausted and as miners struck still deeper, they encountered a more pyritic type of ore, a lot more difficult to work and extract, and poorer in gold content. At Vaalhoek and in the Beta mine there were particularly large quantities of this tough, refractory rock. The establishment of the power-station at Belvedere and of new tube mills greatly improved the speed and efficiency of the extraction process, but as time went by even these failed to compensate for the impoverishment of the ore.

One aspect of the company's operations in these difficult times caused much aggravation, based on misunderstanding among the shareholders: the question of investment in the future – in prospecting. The TGME directors had at an early stage decided to plough back a good percentage of the yearly income into the search for new reefs. They had, after all, acquired in Lionel Phillips's day some 150 000 acres of land with this very purpose in mind. During the 1920s, expenditure on exploration amounted to between £15 000 and £20 000 a year and, despite some grumbling from shareholders, the policy had paid off handsomely. When a new discovery was made, at the Duke's Hill Channel, for instance, or a new extension to the Theta Reef opened up, it very soon recovered the initial outlay.

But in the years following the First World War, despite an exhaustive and sophisticated prospecting programme, the number of new finds declined rapidly. And as profits plunged, so the directors were faced with a dilemma – to abandon the search and concentrate on the working mines, or to continue costly exploration in the face of mounting criticism. In 1923, a year of negligible

profit, the prospecting bill remained at a high £20 000. Although this agitated the shareholders, the board was loath to change its long-held policy. In the following year, after an heroic effort, Barry pushed the total quantity of ore extracted to over 190 000 tons, from which 71 000 ounces of gold were produced, and the books showed a profit of £53 000. But this was a small return relative to the effort. The yield was only six pennyweights to the ton, half that of earlier days. And, to make the situation still more difficult, mining costs rose to offset the benefits of an increasing gold price.

The last months of the 1920s saw the Wall Street crash. The Great Depression was to have long-term repercussions on the world economy. By now the Transvaal Gold Mining Estates faced serious difficulties, and again the spectre of closure loomed. With net profit running at a paltry £3 500 a month, the company was barely able to pay an annual dividend. There were no signs of new discoveries in the field, little prospect of recovery. As the depression deepened, the entire economic structure of the country strained towards breaking point.

Then, in December 1932, came a respite. In that month the finance minister, Havenga, announced that South Africa was to abandon the gold standard. The pound would be allowed to find its own level.

This was the shot-in-the-arm that the mines so desperately needed. The price of gold climbed from 84s. 10d. an ounce to 124s. an ounce. The ratio of working costs to production improved almost overnight, and large areas of hitherto untouched land became exploitable. The tonnage mined rose swiftly, and with it the company's profits. Those for 1933, declared only ninety days after the fixing of the new gold price, amounted to £76 000, and in the following year they had almost doubled, to £151 000. The trend continued. In 1938, a record 300 000 tons of ore were crushed. That year, too, saw the reopening of the Vaalhoek mine, now fitted with watertight doors to prevent flooding.

For the miners of the escarpment, this was the last burst of glory. During the years of the Second World War the plateau of profits continued, and there was a mood of high optimism in the valleys. Mills worked as they had never worked before, spurred on by technical innovation. In 1942, for example, the company installed its own roasting plant, where the local gold – and copper derived from other sources – was treated. It seemed as if the halcyon days were returning.

But the peak had been reached, and was soon to be passed. From then on, as one mine after another became worked out, costs rapidly caught up with and then overtook profits. In 1942 the Pionieskrantz North mine was closed down, and the following year, for the second time, the Vaalhoek mine stopped work. The next to go, in 1945, was the Peach Tree mine. In 1946, the Desire mine closed, though that year brought a last, brief revival of the Vaalhoek, a mine stubbornly reluctant to lie down and die. One of the company's most profitable producers, the Jubilee mine, followed the others in 1947.

The now much-simplified complex of mines was rationalized and streamlined, but by 1951 there was again a marked decline in TGME's returns. The slump continued until, in 1957, the company's chairman, P. H. Anderson, announced a working loss of £2 407. He also warned that the directors were considering the liquidation of the company. In the event, a new company, Corner House Investments, was formed, and bought out TGME's shareholders. Finally, in June 1971, the last mine still in operation, the Beta, put up its shutters.

After generations of pick and shovel, of the clanking of cocopans, the rattle of ore-trains and the roar of the stamp batteries, a deep silence settled over the valley.

While the goldfields of the Witwatersrand prospered as never

Bird life is wonderfully prolific in the indigenous rain-forests of the eastern Transvaal escarpment. Two of the more colourful species found are the Knysna loerie (*opposite page*) and its cousin, the purple-crested loerie (*below*).
Left and below left: aloes glisten in the moisture of early morning at God's Window, a giant cleft on the escarpment's edge that affords a breathtaking view down to the Lowveld below. Sudden and heavy mists are a feature of this grandly mountainous region.

Crossing a drift in the 1920s.

before, their forerunners had been consigned to history. But what of the future? Without the revenue from the mines, what prospects did the area have? Farming, of course, had long been established, the land nurturing maize and tobacco and the renowned local peach trees. But much of the region was sour-veld and poorly suited to agriculture.

It was, however, ideal for forestry and trees filled the gap left by the closure of the mines. Today, the hills of the escarpment and the adjacent Lowveld are cloaked by the largest man-made forests in the world. They cover some 250 000 hectares, of which 85 000 hectares are of a single species, *Pinus patula*. The bulk of the timber is now used in the manufacture of paper, but it was the enthusiasm and involvement of the gold mines which helped to stimulate the original plantings.

When the first prospectors arrived in the middle of the nineteenth century, the escarpment was covered with low indigenous scrub. On higher ground, where the mist belt brought an annual bounty of anything up to sixty inches (1 520 millimetres) of rain, were thick sub-tropical rainforests, and dense stands, too, in the kloofs and valleys along the river courses. With their delicately balanced ecology, these forests were highly vulnerable to invasion by alien species. They were also slow-growing, taking decades to recover after felling. With the demand of the diggers for firewood, and timber for shacks and sluice-boxes, the area in the immediate vicinity of Pilgrim's Rest had become denuded of vegetation within a few years of their arrival. The woodcutters had soon moved farther afield; the hauling of timber to the camp became a profitable business. Then, in the era of the deeper mines, the adits needed a great deal of timber support. Principal source was the ancient yellowwood forests on Belvedere farm, the so-called 'Belvedere Bush'. Thousand of trees were cut there at high contract prices. The sawyers were ruthless in their demands, taking much and returning little. They concentrated on the younger trees, leaving the older and heavier timber, so that the forests had little chance of survival. Soon, vast bare patches began to appear

and spread across the hillsides, bringing with them the devastation of soil erosion.

By the beginning of the century the situation had become critical. In 1903, forestry pioneer Sir David Hutchins toured the area and then, in his Transvaal Forest Report, made urgent recommendations that plantations be started, both to supply the much-needed timber and to relieve the pressure on indigenous trees. He had made a comparative study of the area's climate and those of other countries, finding that the eastern Transvaal most closely resembled Mexico in its weather patterns. Successful afforestation schemes had been launched in Mexico, largely of the pine *Pinus patula*, and he proposed the large-scale planting of the species. The Department of Forestry soon had the first stands of imported Mexican pines growing at Graskop, in what is now the Mac Mac plantation. Perfectly suited to local conditions, the trees rapidly reached maturity. Further species were added, including eucalyptus and two other kinds of pine, *Pinus elliotia* and *Pinus taeda*. Over the next few years, more government plantations were laid out at Barberton, Jessievale and Woodbush.

Meanwhile, the mine managers of TGME had been thinking along similar lines. Shortly after the Anglo-Boer War the company's general manager, Hugh Hugues, decided to plant some wattles within easy reach to provide wood for props. By 1904 he was able to report that some 370 acres of land on the farm Driekop had been ploughed and planted with black and white wattles and with eucalyptus. Hugues estimated the value of the company's 'new asset' at about £6 000 – which, however, he admitted was outrageously optimistic. Nor was anyone else especially hopeful about the outcome of the experiment.

In the event, the results were astonishing. The seedlings grew quickly, and the directors authorized more plantings, though the budget they imposed was strictly limited. They also found an ideal father-figure for their infant schemes in the person of Robert Gardner, hitherto compound manager at the central mines. Gardner was placed in charge of the 'afforestation policy', which became more familiarly known as 'Boss Bob's trees'.

In developing his forests, Gardner encountered a number of problems peculiar to the area: although the soil was generally adequate and the rainfall good, the land was hilly and, in some of the steeper parts, almost impossible to plough. So he introduced the technique of 'pit planting', which was cheaper and appropriate to any gradient.

Gardner also had to contend with a host of natural pests, from locusts and snout beetles to bagworm and *Diplodea pinus* disease. And, of course, there were regular 'Acts of God' – hail and frost, drought and fire. But despite all this, 'Boss Bob's trees' flourished. Large-scale plantings of *Pinus patula* and the swamp pine, *Pinus caribea*, made their appearance. Gardner also introduced cypresses and poplars and, on a smaller scale, experimented with tung oil nut trees.

The first financial yield from the trees appeared in the company's balance-sheet for 1919, and by 1927, with profits amounting to over £29 000, the entire capital cost of the exercise had been recovered.

There was also an impressive improvement in forestry methods. One of the leading sylviculturalists of the time was a Norwegian, Nils Eckbo, who had come to the Union as adviser to the Department of Agriculture but was later offered the post of consultant to the TGME forestry division. Eckbo further rationalized and expanded the tree-planting operation, putting the whole programme on a firm scientific basis. The extent of the plantations doubled, the fire risks greatly reduced, and within a few years, with 40 000 acres planted, the Transvaal Gold Mining Estates had become the country's largest timber company.

All this tended to introduce an element of confusion into the realm of overall policy – a conflict between wood and gold. In

1939 the company negotiated with a Durban concern, the Acme Box Company, to handle TGME's timber output, taking over the extant sawmill and adding one of its own. By now the revenue from the trees had outstripped that from gold, and by the late 1940s profits had risen to over £100 000 a year. Faced with this imbalance, the directors finally decided to divorce the two operations, and a new company, S.A. Forest Investments Ltd, was formed to take over the plantations.

So it was that at the moment when the mines faded into history the area was given a new lease of life. But, as with every kind of progress, there was a price to be paid. The forests cloaked the landscape, and while they were never permitted to encroach on the protected areas of indigenous bush, they effectively prevented the original vegetation from reclaiming the 'Berg. Today, the old character of the escarpment survives only in isolated areas, and in a number of reserves. Among the most remarkable of these is the forest reserve at Mount Sheba.

Mount Sheba is situated on the rim of the plateau, a few kilometres to the south-west of Pilgrim's Rest. Its ragged crest dominates the valley, offering magnificent panoramas of the surrounding countryside. Its highest point, 'Sheba Lookout', rises 700 metres above the village, and on a clear day commands a view of the Lowveld, the Blyde River Canyon, Mariepskop to the north, and the Lebombo Mountains 130 kilometres to the east.

A hundred years ago, this was wild territory, the slopes of the valley watered by a number of streams and thickly wooded with indigenous trees forming a dense, humid rainforest. Elephants browsed among the thickets, and herds of eland, buffalo and kudu roamed the uplands. Lions and leopards stalked the game on the forest fringe. Few people came here, for the woods were all but impenetrable. Among the first to reach the valley were the miners who fanned out from Pilgrim's Creek as the alluvial deposits there became exhausted. They cut a wagon-trail through the rainforest and panned the hidden creeks for gold. To the best of anyone's knowledge, none was ever found, though certainly this was not for want of trying, for the prospectors left their imprint. In the deep shadows of the spectacular Kearney's Creek are the so-called Old Diggings – two of them, 500 metres apart. The tunnels, hewn from the solid rock, are respectively three and six metres deep. Farther down the valley are the remains of the outdoor kitchen of one Hacket, a forlorn, half-overgrown construction of stone slabs set into the red earth of the hillside. Not far from Hacket's kitchen is a third digging, and an impressive one: it reaches 15 metres into the living rock, a testament to the power of the miners' tenacity.

After the diggers had abandoned the Mount Sheba area and moved on, it was turned over to farmland. Three farms, Grootfontein, Concordia and Bendigo Heights, covered the area of today's reserve, and were the property of James Kearney, after whom the creek is named. Born in Dublin in 1886, Kearney became an engineer in the Royal Navy before emigrating to the Transvaal in 1905. There, he married Anna Catharina Pretorius, the great grand-daughter of Voortrekker leader Piet Retief. The Kearneys applied for their farms to be proclaimed as a private nature reserve – the Oribi. On the farm Concordia, they put up a simple wood-and-iron building which they opened as a holiday resort. Given the isolation of the area and their lack of capital, they could do little to develop the idea and, in 1963, after owning the farms for half a century, the couple sold them to I. D. Crabtree. He in turn later sold one of the farms, Bendigo Heights, to the forestry branch of the TGME enterprise, South African Forest Investments, and changed the name of the remaining area to the Mount Sheba Reserve.

It was Crabtree's intention to establish a rest camp comprising a complex of cottages. He made a start, but had managed little more than the foundations of the first when, in March 1968, he sold Mount Sheba to Arthur and Judy Evans. Great-nephew of Sir Arthur Evans, the famed excavator of ancient Knossos in Crete, the new owner decided not only to complete the cottages, but to add a fully-fledged hotel, an idea greeted sceptically by the local residents. The site was so remote and inaccessible at that stage that few people, even in Pilgrim's Rest, were aware of the existence of a nature reserve nearby. But Evans was a determined man, with a passion for ecological preservation and the protection of the rainforests and their denizens. Undaunted, he went ahead, supervising most of the construction himself. By December 1972, against odds ranging from bad roads to a scarcity of building materials, he completed the cottages and the new hotel. The design – a skilful mix of natural stone, thatch, and wood from the surrounding forests – complemented the mood of the valley. A spacious restaurant and a new wing were added.

Development of the hotel and the reserve ran parallel with another of Evans's interests. In 1968, while the first cottages at Mount Sheba were nearing completion, Judy Evans rode across the property and discovered a pocket of countryside in which Transvaal proteas were growing in abundance. An enthusiastic amateur, she began to introduce a few Cape proteas, and the plants took kindly to their new habitat, the first coming to flower in 1974. The hobby became a commercial enterprise, and by 1978 some 8 000 bushes were flourishing in the reserve.

Running both hotel and protea farm, however, proved too onerous, so in 1982 the Evanses sold the hotel and concentrated on the latter enterprise. The hotel was taken over by Ovland Limited, a property development division of the Ovenstone Investments Group. The new owners decided to upgrade it, and to increase the number of cottages from the original ten. The modern complex comprises a luxury hotel, complete with every amenity and comfort (including a splendid cuisine) which nevertheless blends perfectly with its surroundings.

Set on the crest of the ridge which runs down the valley's centre, few hotels can be blessed with a more majestic setting. From high on the edge of the plateau above, the road branches off from the main road a few kilometres from the start of Pilgrim's Hill and, following part of an old wagon-trail – once an alternative route from Lydenburg to Pilgrim's Rest – snakes down to the hotel in its enclave of trees. To step from here or from one of the cottages into the nearby rainforest is to enter another world, twilit and primaeval, filled with the rustle and stir of hidden life.

In technical terms, the forest at Mount Sheba is described as being in 'climax condition', which means that the trees are allowed to mature and to die of old age, protected from outside threat, including the intrusion of alien vegetation. The edges of the forest are guarded by a pioneer growth of ancient yellowwoods, many estimated to be over 1 500 years old. Altogether, some 105 tree species were identified during a study carried out by the students of the Moss Herbarium in Johannesburg. Many of the more important ones have been tagged where they occur along the network of paths which explore the reserve from Kearney's Creek, with its old diggings, to the Trout and Aloe Pools and the many waterfalls, the Gola Gola Falls and Marco's Mantle being among the most charming.

If the larger animals have long since gone, many smaller species live their secret lives in the undergrowth. Among the antelopes found here are oribi, klipspringer, blesbok and the grey rhebuck. Monkeys chatter in the high branches of the trees, and a host of bird life adds its voice to the sounds of the forest. Over a hundred different species of bird, from the Knysna loerie to the Cape canary, from mousebirds to rock thrushes, waxbills and white-eyes, have been spotted here. All this combines to create a fascinating and intricate ecology, a living picture of the escarpment as it was for many thousands of years – of Africa before man set his hand upon it.

Two studies of the Aloe Pools at Mount Sheba. Much of the region's natural vegetation has been destroyed, supplanted by the pines and eucalyptus trees that now comprise the world's largest man-made woodlands. But in the wilder uplands the original plant life – trees and scrub, ericas and proteas and a proliferation of aloes – remains relatively untouched by man. There are about a hundred species of indigenous tree in the Mount Sheba reserve.

Another kind of wealth

Around the turn of the century a British military officer with an interest in angling introduced trout into the streams of the eastern Transvaal. It was to prove a rewarding piece of enterprise.

Trout are not indigenous to Africa, but they had already been successfully imported to stock rivers in the Cape, and it was from this source that he obtained ova. Over the next few decades a number of enthusiastic amateurs bred trout in home-made hatching boxes and distributed them in the local rivers. They flourished, for these fish enjoy clear, cold, fast-running, high mountain streams. As anglers flocked to the area, demand rose for larger stock, and in 1949 the Transvaal Fisheries Institute was established on the outskirts of Lydenburg. Today, the Institute breeds many thousands of fish each year, including other game-species such as vlei kurper and large-mouth bass, all of which have been introduced into the public angling waters stretching from the Sabie River to the Blyde River at Pilgrim's Rest. Thus began a major attraction to the area, one which has contributed significantly to the growth of tourism – the escarpment's third major industry along with farming and forestry.

This was the start of the region's thriving tourist industry.

Predictably, the focus of attention for most visitors is Pilgrim's Rest itself. After the last mine, the Beta, closed in 1971, there was a time during which the future of the village hung in the balance. Then, in 1974, it was sold in its entirety, by Rand Mine Properties, to the Transvaal Provincial Administration which undertook, through its Museum Service, to restore its early, uniquely charming character.

Much has been achieved in the past decade; much remains to be done. For most visitors, the starting point is the older part of the village, with its zinc-and-wood houses strung out along the road which winds down the valley (curiously, in an area where almost every donga is identified, this main thoroughfare, used by uncounted thousands of miners, has never been given a name). An Information Centre directs the newcomer to the various places of interest. In the upper village, for example, is the House Museum. One of the old prefabricated homes, restored to the condition at the time of its erection in the 1880s, the museum is stark in its simplicity, providing a sharp insight into the frugality of the average miner's life. It is complemented by the neat, pocket-handkerchief garden at the back, complete with chicken-run, open-air oven and marshalled rows of vegetables, overlooking the scarred and battered banks of the creek.

In the nature of things the early community, cut off as it was from the outside world for so long, had to be as self-reliant as possible. The village store thus played a key role. Across the way from the House Museum is a restoration of a typical shop of the period: L. Dredzen & Co, a place authentic in every detail. All the necessities of pioneer life are here, from beans and mealie-meal to nails and bolts, from sugar, tea and coffee to such miner's requisites as picks and shovels; mining-lamps, and even explosives. A major stock item was the patent medicine, each brand tried and trusted: Lennon's Dutch medicine including 'Doepa', 'Spijkerbalsem' and 'Duiwelsdrek'; Allenbury's Throat Pastilles; Beecham's Pills for stomach complaints, and Virata Brain and Nerve Tonic. Some labels claim to cure more than one ailment. One kind of health syrup, for example, was something of a panacea, the answer to everything from liver complaints to anaemia, dizziness, sleeplessness and bad breath.

One medicine, however, ranked above all others in the pioneering days. Gold and strong liquor were inseparable companions. In the rugged first years the local *cantinas* had been crude, make-shift affairs, thrown together from tin and packing-cases and as often as not open to the sky. But from the time that Benjamin launched his company in the 1880s, drinking took on a new style. Permanent hotels made their appearance. Leading the bucolic band was the famed Royal, still a focal point: it began its brisk business in about 1885, and has never looked back. Filled with period furniture, it faithfully preserves its Victorian origins. One of the main features is the old bar, which has its own curious history: apparently it was once a small Roman Catholic mission church at Delagoa Bay. When the chapel became too small to hold its congregation, it was sold off to the owner of the Royal, who had it transported by ox-wagon over the 'Berg to Pilgrim's Rest, erected as part of his hotel, and dedicated to Dionysus.

Despite the wealth extracted from the ground, there was little luxury in Pilgrim's Rest. However, a solitary island of opulence survives, in the shape of the Alanglade House Museum, situated across the Blyde River. For fourteen years it was the home of Dick Barry, managing director of TGME mines, his wife Gladys and their seven children. Named after two of the latter, Alan and Gladys, it was designed to the Barrys' requirements by the noted architect Sir Herbert Baker. It is Edwardian affluence at its most attractive, its rooms furnished with elements of later periods, in lavish Art Nouveau and Art Deco styles. There is a large living-room, a smoking-room, two entertainment rooms, two nurseries for the children (one for the day, the other for the night), a school-room, and quarters for the staff, who included a governess, a nursemaid, a cook and a driver. The gardens are spacious and include a separate rose garden, vegetable garden, a croquet lawn, tennis court and swimming pool.

All this was a far cry from the primitive life of the first Pilgrim's Creek miners. Little now remains of the days of Wheelbarrow Alec and the first flood of raw, tangle-bearded prospectors, plunging down the valley to fossick furiously and to set up their swarming complex of claims, sluice-boxes and tents. The Museum Service, however, has reconstructed a section of the old diggings, a short distance from the upper village. Here there are three claims, complete with tents, wattle-and-daub shacks and sluice-boxes. Nearby is the 'Glory Hole', an early mine burrowed under a colossal rock, one of the first 'treasure chests' of gold to be discovered. To complete the picture, the Museum stages panning demonstrations by Claude Cogill. From old Pilgrim's Rest stock, Claude spent many years working his profitable Mac Mac claim before retiring to the village to show visitors how men like his grandfather, one of the first diggers in the valley, made their hard-won livelihood.

Panning demonstrations represent one end of the mining spectrum; the other can be viewed during a tour around the TGME reduction works farther down the valley, on a site overlooking the Blyde River. These, too, are in the course of being restored, though the work is still far from complete.

Here is a picture of mining technology in the years just before and after the turn of the century. Besides the reduction works, the complex includes a re-electrified section of the old ore-railway, laboratories for geological research, assay offices, workshops for the repair and maintenance of the machinery, and blacksmiths' and farriers' shops where the company's donkeys and mules were shod and fed.

The Beta mine is also being restored, though the task has proved far from simple. Its tunnels have collapsed in a number of places and, while this may have been a reality of mining life in the past, it is hardly likely to encourage present-day visitors!

For all its rigours, the life of a Pilgrim's Rest miner was filled with sturdy cheerfulness and optimism. Other areas of the Drakensberg escarpment, however, trace a darker story. At Andries-Ohrigstad, for instance, there are lingering memories of the trials and suffering of the first Voortrekkers to establish a presence in the region. Long deserted, the village revived as an agricultural centre after the menace of malaria had been eradicated. Today it is situated a few kilometres from its original site, of which almost nothing remains but a few forlorn relics. Some 33 metres of the defence wall of the fort built by that compulsive Trekker Hendrik Potgieter still stand among the quiet fields. The dry-stone wall is topped with a layer of compacted mud in which apertures were left as firing points for defence against marauding Pedi. The local tribesmen, though, took third place in the litany of the Trekkers' tribulations – after the plague and their own insatiable appetite for dissension. A short distance away is the Ohrigstad cemetery, the graveyard preserved, and a memorial to the plague victims erected. Nearby stands a tomb, designed in the shape of an ox-wagon, which contains fragments of the headstones of Koos 'Lawaai' Burger, Potgieter's arch-enemy, and the others who died in that terrible summer of 1848.

By then, the schismatics had fled from the dying town to form a new settlement of their own, 45 kilometres to the south, beyond the sickness belt. They remembered their sufferings in its name, Lydenburg. Later, during the constitutional upheavals of the 1850s, the eastern Trekkers enjoyed a fleeting independence as 'De Republiek Lydenburg en Zuid-Afrika'. Today, the town's municipal crest tells its story: it has quarterings showing an ox-wagon, a wheat-sheaf, the head of a kudu, and a prospector's pick, shovel, pan and accompanying gold nugget.

There are many places in this pleasant country town redolent of its history, but a synoptic view can be enjoyed at the Lydenburg Museum. Its wide variety of exhibits ranges from Stone Age masks and cave relics found in the mountains nearby to records of the Voortrekkers and pictures of the Lydenburg Commando during the Anglo-Boer War. Not far away are architectural memorials to the pioneer days: the simple thatched and whitewashed Voortrekker school and the first Dutch Reformed Church in the territory, situated on the corner of Church and Kantoor streets. Then there is the old powder magazine on Viljoen Street, built with bricks taken from the British 'Fort Mary' after the siege of 1880, and still bearing the graffiti inscribed by the English soldiers. For those who appreciate graceful architecture, the Loreto Convent is well worth a visit. The building was started by five pioneer nuns who arrived by ox-wagon from Pretoria, and was completed in 1898. Two storeys high, it is surmounted by a bell-tower. Its front garden is enhanced by a stately row of palm trees.

One of the main 'exhibits' of the Anglo-Boer War period in Lydenburg is outside the town. The famed Long Tom Pass is the highest motor-road in the country, running eastwards from Lydenburg to the rim of the escarpment and thence down to Sabie and the Lowveld beyond. The road had long been in use before the war, for it was part of the 'Ou Hawepad' to the coast, and featured such well-known outspans as Whisky Creek and the Old Trading Post. Whisky Creek's name is especially apt, for in the high days of the transport-riders 'liquid gold' was sold there at the equivalent of 90 cents a bottle. But its finest hour came in early September 1900 with the Boers' fighting retreat up the Pass. Where the road dips down below the lip of the plateau, you can see the Long Tom siege-gun's last position and, not far away, one of the craters left by an exploding shell. Farther on are the precipitous Devil's Knuckles, where thirteen Boer wagons were sent tumbling down in the dusk of the final withdrawal.

At Sabie, with its sawmills and winding railway line, the visitor finds himself in the heart of forest country. Besides its fine Anglican Church, designed by Sir Herbert Baker and built in 1913, there is a comprehensive Forestry Museum which features displays on the history of the region's plantations and on the different species: pines, eucalyptus, yellowwood. The Department of Forestry and the private companies – principally Mondi, the paper company which owns the forests – have taken care to preserve as well as they are able the indigenous flora and fauna within their boundaries. Many wildlife species are not able to survive in the plantations, but others – baboons, porcupines, and small predators such as mongoose and serval – have taken up residence without complaint. Some of the flora, including proteas, the red hot pokers (*Kniphophia* spp.), *Erica cerinthoides* and cycads (*Encephalartus* spp.) are also carefully protected.

Pride of the area is its rivers, and their many beautiful waterfalls, all of which are worth a visit. They include the Sabie, the

Lydenburg's second church (foreground) which has also served as a school, a church hall and a bank, has been graced with the addition of gables and brightened with plaster. The town's present church (background) contains yellowwood beams which are the only surviving remnants of the NG Kerk erected at the first, ill-fated Trekker settlement of Andries-Ohrigstad.

A myriad small streams and rivers course down the high and verdant slopes of the eastern Transvaal escarpment, their paths charmingly interrupted by quiet pools and a wealth of waterfalls, some tumbling down the open mountainside; others, like the spectacular Marco's Mantle *(left)*, hidden among the forest glades of the Mount Sheba Reserve. *Top right:* the cool cascade of Aloe Pools. *Above right:* light and shade in Kearney's Creek.

New Chum, the Horse Shoe, the Lisbon and the Berlin falls. The Sabie River is especially notable for the excellence of its trout fishing. Water conservation is also a concern of the forestry officials: trees are planted no closer than twenty metres from a stream, and alien vegetation is kept away from the watercourses and waterfalls.

If angling is a serene, contemplative way of spending a holiday, there are other, more strenuous activities on offer, including the local walks and hikes. Some of these, at Mount Sheba, for example, are in privately owned areas, but there are six public hiking trails around the escarpment which allow one a fine view of its upland splendours. In ascending order of difficulty, they are the Yellowwood trail, the Protea trail, the Morgenzon trail, the Prospector's trail, the Blyde River Canyon trail, and the Fanie Botha trail.

The first of these, the Yellowwood, is an ideal beginner's course. It is 24 kilometres long and takes a comfortable two days. Starting at the Bourke's Luck potholes, it follows the Belvedere Valley before descending to the Mount Hebron plateau, where the hiker is rewarded with a panoramic view over the Blyde River Canyon. After an overnight stop at the end of the trail, the second day retraces the way back to Bourke's Luck potholes.

From Bourke's Luck, too, begins the four-day, 40-kilometre Protea trail, which again follows the Belvedere Valley before turning aside through the indigenous forests leading to Op-de-Berg, near the Devil's Window.

About the same length as the Protea is the circular Morgenzon trail, which begins and ends at the Morgenzon Forest Station. On the way it takes in a representative selection of indigenous forest, pine plantation and open grassland, where one can see grey rhebuck, oribi and sometimes – a bonus, this – a herd of wild horses, believed to be the descendants of those of the early gold diggers.

The recently-opened Prospector's trail, 65 kilometres long, calls for prospector's legs plus a stout pair of boots. It begins at the Mac Mac Forest Station, climbs up by the Bonnet Pass near Graskop, following the route used by the miners, and then dips down into Pilgrim's Rest, stopping at an authentic miner's hut at the edge of the village. From there it goes by the old Columbia mine to the Morgenzon Forest Station and Black Hill before finishing at Bourke's Luck. The route offers sweeping views to distant Wolkberg, Strydpoort and Waterberg.

The five-day Blyde River Canyon trail is about the same length as the Prospector's. As its name suggests, it explores the magnificent 26 000 hectares of the Blyde River Canyon Reserve. Beginning near Graskop, at God's Window, it follows the course of the Blyde River to Bourke's Luck before descending to the floor of the canyon, reaching the Blyde Canyon hut in the public resort. From there the trail leads to the Kadishi Valley where, at Swadini, is found one of the reserve's unique features: a 'tufa' waterfall. The water here, flowing down from the dolomitic strata above, is rich in calcium. Heavy growths of moss in the falls extract carbon dioxide from the water through photosynthesis, which creates characteristic deposits of smooth, caramel-coloured limestone, or 'tufa', on the rocks.

From Swadini, the trail goes on to the Blyde Canyon Dam in the Sybrand van Niekerk Public Resort. This is an interesting and highly rewarding trail (for those hardier souls who enjoy footslogging) for it offers the hiker a variety of climatic conditions, geological formations – including some dizzying perspectives up the millions of years' of rock strata in the canyon – and an abundance of wildlife. Animal species include antelope, porcupine, serval and caracal. The flora is richly varied, ranging from wild orchids through Cape beech to baobab trees. Otters can sometimes be glimpsed along the banks of the river. There are three species of loerie in the reserve, which is also one of the few remaining habitats of the rare bald ibis.

Of the six trails, the longest is the five-day, 76,9-kilometre Fanie Botha, which starts at the Ceylon State Forest and follows a route through pine plantations and indigenous bush, the latter broken by stretches of grassland where the hiker may spot antelope, including oribi, bushbuck, duiker, rhebuck and klipspringer. Among many species of trees, the forest here is home to white stinkwood, ironwood, lemonwood and yellowwood. The trail takes in the Mac Mac Falls before ending, in a fitting climax, with the view across the Lowveld from God's Window.

These are just a few of the delights that the 'Berg offers the visitor. There are of course many other walks and drives, including those to the Echo Caves, north of Ohrigstad, and to the Sudwala Caves, near Nelspruit, with their fantasia of stalactites and stalagmites – many weighing several tons – and the fossils of *Collenia*, a primitive form of seaweed, on the roof of one of the chambers. Visits to places farther afield might include the great valley of De Kaap and Barberton, with its statue of Jock of the Bushveld in FitzPatrick Park. This is only one of the memorials to the famous dog, for the surmised route taken by Jock and his master is marked by a number of bronze plaques – near Pretorius Kop, at the Numbi Gate of the Kruger Park, on the farm Peebles, at Sabie, Spitskop and Graskop (the 'Paradise Camp' of the transportriders), at Mac Mac, at Pilgrim's Rest, on the crest of Pilgrim's Hill, at Steenkamp Bridge, at Krugerspost (scene of the epic battle with the baboon on a pole) and at Lydenburg. Mining relics are not confined to Pilgrim's Rest, but dot the area – at Bourke's Luck, for instance, where part of the old minehead and mine buildings still survive.

Thus the gold may have gone from the valleys, but there is other wealth to be found and carried away by today's visitor. There is history in the hills and valleys, and in the minds of the people of the area. This is a warm and hospitable community, and the old-timers of Pilgrim's Rest, in particular, are never short of a story – men such as Claude Cogill and the inimitable Mike Owens, who have decades of mining experience behind them. They need little encouragement to bring back the past, with all its excitement and adventure, and to resurrect the ghosts of the characters who played out the human drama – and comedy – on the early stage.

The portrait gallery could scarcely be more varied: Louis Trichardt and the fiery Hendrik Potgieter; President Burgers and Theophilus Shepstone; the litigious Irish journalist Phelan and Tommy Dennison with his wooden pistols. And, of course, there is the polyglot cast of ordinary miners, from Wheelbarrow Alec to French Bob, from Elizabeth Russell, up to her knees in the mud of Pilgrim's Creek, to 'The Bosun', Matthias Mockett, himself. On foot with pick and shovel over their shoulder, on horseback or by oxwagon, with hope springing eternal in their hearts, they seem to throng the valleys still.

And when the happy pilgrim of today loads up his own wagon and takes his leave of the 'Berg, they go with him.

The splendours of the Mount Sheba region, a few kilometres to the west of Pilgrim's Rest. *Right:* the rising tiers of the Transvaal Drakensberg escarpment.

Parts of the Mount Sheba Reserve and surrounding countryside are home to flourishing pockets of Transvaal proteas. In 1968 Judy Evans, wife of Arthur Evans, who built the hotel and developed the nature reserve, stumbled across one such concentration. A keen horticulturalist, she began to introduce a few Cape proteas to the area. These thrived, and within a decade some 8 000 plants were gracing the upland region – a successful and environmentally worthwhile commercial venture: the plants complement the marvellous wealth of other indigenous species of the escarpment.
Below: Protea neriifolia. Right and opposite page: the king protea, *P. cynaroides,* mingling with helichrysums.
Bottom left and right: the head of a budding *Leucadendron salignum.*

Mount Sheba's floral paradise. Included among the indigenous trees of the area are splendid yellowwoods and black ironwoods, colourful wild peaches and wild lemons, and the more intriguingly named silky barks, cabbage trees, bastard ironwoods, notsungs, poison olives – and bachelor's refuge, whose smooth curved branches rise up beyond a maiden's presumed reach. Some of the plants, such as the ferns and cycads, are of ancient origin. *Opposite page:* part of the primeval forest at Mount Sheba, affording a glimpse of the kind of terrain over which the early explorers and prospectors had to find their way. *Left:* flower head of the succulent shrub *Crassula ribucunda. Below:* leaves of a young *Faurea saligna*, the Transvaal beechwood or 'boekenhout'. *Below left: Selago* sp. *Bottom left:* wild asparagus *(Protasparagus angusticladus). Bottom right: Plectrunthus* sp. and fern in the heart of the forest.
Overleaf: Marco's Mantle, set against a backcloth of indigenous forest.

Pilgrim's Rest, a few kilometres from Mount Sheba, was born in 1873, when a character known as Wheelbarrow Alec – he carried his worldly possessions around in a barrow – found gold in a creek on the western side of the 'Berg's edge. The consequent rush of diggers, from as far afield as Australia and California, lasted three frantic years, and many fine nuggest were recovered from the stream and from nearby Waterfall Gulley and Peach Tree Creek. In 1875 the area produced an impressive £200 000-worth of the yellow metal, including the 6 038-gram Reward Nugget. The following year, though, the 'easy' gold of the gravels began to run out, companies were formed to mine the deeper levels and the era of the lone pick-and-shovel digger, of canvas home and packing-case canteen,

gave way to a more stable period of organized mining activity, for the most part under the management of Transvaal Gold Mining Estates Limited. This lasted a full five decades, until the seams approached exhaustion and the company turned most of its attention and efforts to afforestation. The village of Pilgrim's Rest, however, still retains its early character, many of its old buildings meticulously preserved.

Above: a panoramic view of the town and its lovely surrounds.

Opposite page bottom: some of the prefabricated houses so characteristic of the early settlement. This row includes the offices of the *Pilgrim's Rest and Sabie News.*

Left: the village viewed from the ridge to the north, with a kiepersol, or cabbage tree, in the foreground.

Pilgrim's Rest potpourri. *Clockwise from below:* a craft shop that makes and sells karakul rugs; typical period buildings; aloes and crassulas sprawling across sun-warmed rocks close to the village; the indigenous and very poisonous 'gifbol', a tumbleweed whose generic name *Boophane* translates as 'slaughterer of cattle'; cottages of wood and iron, many of them occupied by retired miners, line the dusty and still unnamed road through the village. *Left:* Pilgrim's Rest wakes slowly to its undemanding life in the early morning light.

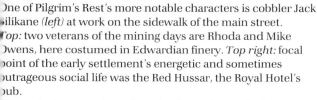

One of Pilgrim's Rest's more notable characters is cobbler Jack Silikane *(left)* at work on the sidewalk of the main street. *Top:* two veterans of the mining days are Rhoda and Mike Owens, here costumed in Edwardian finery. *Top right:* focal point of the early settlement's energetic and sometimes outrageous social life was the Red Hussar, the Royal Hotel's pub.

Above: the bar served as a location for an SABC television series; Grethe Fox, one of its stars, is seen here during filming. *Below right:* John Mkhonto winds up the gramophone in 'The Enterprising Store' – L. Dredzen & Co., which stocked everything from dried peas to explosives.

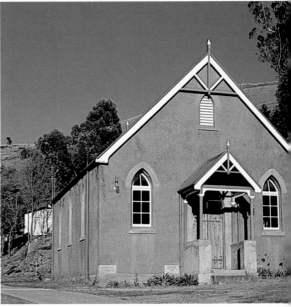

Preservation and restoration. *Clockwise from above:* one of the
curio shops that contributes to Pilgrim's Rest's income; the clay
oven in Tommy Broadhurst's cottage, now the Miner's House
Museum, which overlooks the stream and the old workings;
a young girl's bedroom, one of the features of the Museum; the
dining room of the Museum, with caretaker Eddie Maluka, at
eighty-six a strong contender for Oldest Inhabitant, on duty;
Victorian utensils and crockery in the Museum's kitchen; the
Methodist church, overlooking the village; the famed
Robber's Grave, in the Pilgrim's Rest cemetery. As a mark of
sustained posthumous disapproval, it was set at right angles to
the surrounding graves.
Overleaf: the Royal Hotel, pride of Pilgrim's Rest.

Above: Alanglade House, once the opulent home of Transvaal Gold Mining Estates' general manager R.A. Barry and his wife Gladys. It was designed by the renowned architect Sir Herbert Baker in the early years of the century, and is now a museum, reflecting Edwardian affluence at its most attractive. *Right:* Alanglade's spacious entrance hall and staircase. *Opposite page, clockwise from top left:* hunting trophies adorn a wall in the museum; the elegant dining room; Gladys Barry's writing desk; the bedroom of one of the seven Barry children. The house boasted two nurseries, a schoolroom, a large withdrawing room, a smoking room and two reception rooms.

Top left: local resident Fred Briggs stands beside the Glory Hole, one of the most profitable of the early Pilgrim's Rest workings. It is at the upper end of the village. *Top right:* the Beta Mine was one of the last to be closed down – it finally ceased production in 1971. Pictured is one of the adits.
Above: some of the Beta's mining rigs now do duty as trellisses for flowering creepers.
Right: overgrown scars of the old diggings.

Left: gold-panning demonstrations are regularly held at Pilgrim's Rest. The old claims were about 50 metres square; running water was essential for recovery of the gold from the gravel, which sometimes lay a full six metres below ground. Diggers in the upper reaches used up most of the water; those working lower down were obliged to devise ingenious irrigation schemes, building 'races' linking their claims to other watercourses flowing higher up the mountainside. *Below:* a collection of gold nuggets, of the kind that sustained the dreams of the early miners. *Bottom:* a cross-section of gold-bearing ore extracted from the Beta Mine.

Below: the service hoist for the cocopan trucks that brought ore from the mine to the reduction works at Pilgrim's Rest.
Right: cocopans at the crusher plant.

Below: an ore-crushing mill. *Left:* a drill-handle at the reduction works. *Bottom:* a general view of the reduction works which, like all of Pilgrim's Rest, is being systematically restored.
Overleaf: an avenue of plane trees near Mount Sheba.

Around the turn of the century an enterprising British military officer introduced trout into the eastern Transvaal's streams. Over the decades the fish – which are not indigenous to Africa but had been successfully bred at the Cape – flourished in the clear, cold mountain waters, providing an extra dimension to the region's tourist attractions. More recently, the Transvaal Fisheries Institute has bred and distributed other game-species, including vlei kurper and large-mouth bass. *Right:* Mike Owens, the personification of angling contentment, casts for early morning trout in the Blyde River.
Below: the Joubert Bridge, named after a one-time mining commissioner, spans the Blyde River below Pilgrim's Rest.
Opposite page: the Blyde River seen from the Joubert Bridge.

Right: the pine-clad undulations of the high ground north of Robber's Pass. *Opposite page, top:* the Kaspersnek area was host to one of the earliest of the Voortrekker expeditions; *centre:* dense plantations flank the steep road that winds down steeply from Robber's Pass to Pilgrim's Rest; *bottom:* a parade of pine trees stands to attention along one side of the Pilgrim's Rest golf course. The course has been laid out on one of the region's very few fairly flat stretches of land. *Overleaf:* the golf course on a frosty winter's morning.

The Belvedere power station (*opposite page*) was in its day one of the modern marvels of the area. A central 60-stamp mill, linked to the mines by a twelve-kilometre railway system, was constructed in the late 1890s, which prompted the enlargement of the modest and somewhat unreliable (it depended on the vagaries of the Blyde River's flow) station that had previously served the miners. The new plant involved the cutting of a four-kilometre water-race from higher up the river. Long since shut down, the Belvedere power station survives as a silent showpiece of fine Victorian industrial architecture. *Left:* the power station's control panel. *Below:* one of its generators.

Top: the spectacular cliffs of the Blyde River Canyon seen from a point above the Belvedere power station. *Left:* the skeletal victim of a veld fire.
Above: the old hydro station, now tree-enclosed and idle.
Opposite page: power-lines rise steeply to the crest of the escarpment, linking the valley to the outside world.

Near the confluence of the Blyde and Treur rivers a small but very profitable gold mine known as Bourke's Luck operated until quite recent times. *Right:* the now-abandoned mine's ore-crusher. *Above:* clarifiers at the mine's reduction works.

Opposite page, left: a natural fern garden at Bourke's Luck pot-holes, which are striking examples of water-induced erosion; *top right:* the Treur River has cleaved a deep passage through the rock on its way to join the Blyde. The names respectively mean 'sorrowful' and 'joyful', commemorating a Voortrekker expedition's presumed loss and its later, happy, return; *bottom right:* running water has sculpted fantastic shapes along the Treur's ravine.

Overleaf: lowering clouds over the Lowveld near God's Window.

The area's aboriginal inhabitants were the Bushmen, or Khoisan, long since displaced. But there are a great many relics of Bushman occupation, such as these examples of their wonderful rock art *(right and centre right)*, in the caves and rock shelters *(bottom)* of the region, most of which have clear views over land that once teemed with game. *Below: Aloe arborescens growing in a rock crevice.*

The smaller delights of the eastern Transvaal. Two of the myriad plant species are *Nerine angustifolia*, or ribbon-leafed nerina *(above left)*, whose rose-coloured flowerheads bloom in late summer; and *Lilium longiflorum (above)*, a species of Asiatic origin which has taken readily to the escarpment region. This one was photographed on the roadside near Lisbon Falls. *Centre left:* a long-gone prospector's beacon stands lonely in the evening light. *Below:* Waterval Spruit, near Graskop.

An old photograph *(right)* of the Zeederberg Coach after its conversion from mule-power to motor-power, together with its proud owner, Robinson Wood Richardson, and an assortment of passengers. *Below right and below:* old and new – the original Kowyn's Pass, and the pass of today, a modern covered highway completed in 1962.

Bottom left: Claude Cogill, renowned old-timer of Mac Mac and Pilgrim's Rest and one of the few surviving professional prospectors. *Jock of the Bushveld* is one of South Africa's classic stories and this plaque *(bottom right)* is one of the many marking the route followed by the author, Percy FitzPatrick, and his redoubtable dog.

The escarpment has so many features that catch and hold the eye, but few are lovelier than its waterfalls, ranging from the Sabi through the charming Lisbon and Berlin to the magnificence of the double falls of Mac Mac, plunging a full 65 metres into the gorge below. Almost all of them are surrounded by a profusion of plant life, natural gardens of moss and fern and dense growths of indigenous tree and bush. *Bottom:* the striking face of the Graskop Falls. *Below:* maidenhair fern (*Adiantum* sp.) flourishes in the damp air around Lisbon Creek. *Left:* tangled indigenous scrub clings to the precipitous sides of The Pinnacle, near Graskop.
Overleaf, left: the outline of the 'Madonna and Child' rock formation can be seen through the cascading curtain of the Lisbon Falls; *right:* spectacular aerial view of the Lisbon Falls.

A living landmark, George Marshall *(right and below)* is one of the best-known of the surviving prospectors. He stands, at right, with his dog Teddy in front of Billy Davis's cave. Here, in 1884, Billy and his wire-haired terrier defended themselves against a party of marauders. *Below right:* a furnace near Lisbon Creek, once used to smelt the cyanide amalgam solution used in the gold extraction process. The forest is slowly taking over most of the old workings.
Opposite page: Goedgeloof sawmill, near Bourke's Luck, an area that has long been a centre of timber production.

Mac Mac Pools – one of the most charming spots in the escarpment region. Alluvial gold was discovered in the river in 1873 by one Johannes Muller, prompting a rush of diggers from far and wide. The curious name given to the mining camp, and to the twin waterfalls and the pools, derives from the number of Scotsmen in the first, rugged community of miners. The pools are enjoyed by swimmers as well as sightseers; there are changing rooms, picnic and braai sites and, two kilometres along the road, a fine view of the Mac Mac Falls themselves. *Left:* tree ferns fringe the cool tranquility of the pools. *Below:* an abstract pattern of pebbles in the crystal-clear waters.

The escarpment region is a paradise for hikers.
Above: a party on the Fanie Botha Trail, part of an enticing network of scenic hiking ways and nature walks. *Far left:* an overnight hut on the trail, near Mac Mac. *Centre left:* taking a breather en route. *Left:* sunrise at the Mac Mac Falls.
Overleaf: the Blyde River gorge and its guardians, the Three Rondavels.

Trees have taken over where gold left off. The mines have long since been closed, but the hills of the escarpment and the adjacent Lowveld nurture the largest man-made forests in the world, covering some 250 000 hectares, of which 85 000 hectares are of a single species, *Pinus patula.* The home of an early settler, Henry Thomas Glynn (a farmer and big-game hunter turned gold-miner, and known as the Squire of Sabie) is being converted into the new Sabie Forestry Museum. Featured on these pages are some of the showpiece relics of the pioneering era. *Below left:* a sylvan study. *Bottom:* the entrance to the Anglican Church at Sabie, designed by Sir Herbert Baker.

Right and below: the lovely Sabie Falls. The nearby town of Sabie owes its origins to a curious tale of inadvertant prospecting. In 1895 landowner H.T. Glynn and his son (also H.T.) entertained friends to a lively picnic lunch at the Klein Sabie Falls, after which hosts and guests indulged in some shooting practice. Their targets were empty bottles placed on a ledge; the bullets scored the rock face, revealing traces of gold. The Glynn mining operation flourished, despite enormous technical problems, and by the time it closed down, in 1950, nearly a million and a quarter ounces had been extracted – and the settlement had become a thriving little centre, born of gold and sustained, later, by the giant afforestation schemes launched in the region.

Cascades of beauty. Some of the waterfalls of the Sabie and adjacent regions are the Bridal Veil *(left, below and opposite page, right)*, the Lone Creek *(opposite page, top left)* and the Horse Shoe *(opposite page, bottom left)*.
Overleaf: the 'living' tufa waterfall, with its characteristic caramel-coloured deposits, at the F.H. Odendaal camp in the Blydepoort Public Resort.

The Long Tom Pass *(left and above)*, named after the heavy Creusot siege guns used so effectively against the British during an Anglo-Boer War skirmish, is the highest motorway in the country. *Top left:* replica of the Long Tom. *Top right:* a forestry lookout station on the Pass.

The escarpment region is notable for the number and impressive extent of the caverns and natural corridors that the waters of millennia have carved into its dolomite rock formations. Two of the most renowned such complexes are the Echo and the Sudwala caves. *Top left:* Seroto Mohlala is one of the Echo's guides, explaining its wonders in an incongruous Texan drawl (the product of his years spent showing Transatlantic visitors the sights). *Top right and centre left:* flowstone formations decorate the walls of the Echo Caves. *Above left:* this root of a *Ficus* tree (the species is believed to have the longest root of any of the earth's plants) penetrates the roof of one of the caves. *Above right:* one of the many chambers of the Sudwala Caves. *Opposite page:* the firing port of the old Voortrekker fort at Andries-Ohrigstad, built for defence against hostile Pedi.

Right: the Abel Erasmus Pass was completed in 1959 and includes the J.G. Strijdom tunnel, named in honour of a former prime minister of South Africa. *Below:* a group of youngsters put on an impromptu show for the camera.
Opposite page, top: this homestead near Ohrigstad once belonged to Abel Erasmus, after whom the nearby Pass was named. *Below left:* a show-stealing Ohrigstad cyclist at the top of Robber's Pass.
Centre right: sorting tobacco – one of the region's more important crops – at Ohrigstad.
Bottom right: Abel Erasmus's farm, with its backcloth of autumn-tinged syringas.

131

The Lydenburg area – indeed much of the entire escarpment region – is something of a mecca for anglers, contributing to a tourist industry that, after farming and forestry, is the area's third largest. Increasing demand from the angling fraternity led, in 1949, to the establishment of the Transvaal Fisheries Institute on the outskirts of Lydenburg.
Left: netting mature trout, for spawning, at the De Kuilen Trout Hatchery. *Above, from far left:* Frans Maphonga and his helper, Abram Sekgobela, two of the hatchery's staff, strip the eggs from a rainbow trout; the next step in the fertilization process is to strip sperm onto the ova; following this the fertilized ova are washed and then sorted – after about 25 days, at the 'eye' stage. *Top right:* the end result – the yolk sac fry, or alevins.

The escarpment region was once the haunt of the big predators, driven away, from about the mid-nineteenth century, by the encroachment of man, leaving the field to their smaller and less obtrusive cousins. *Above:* the serval cat *(Felis serval)* is mainly nocturnal, its prey a variety of wildlife ranging from rodents and lizards to small buck. *Top:* the shy, thick-tailed bush-baby *(Galago crassicaudatus)* is also nocturnal, feeding on roosting birds, fruit, berries and insects. *Right:* flowering grasses on the escarpment.

134

Other mammals of the region include the large-spotted genet *(Genetta tigrina) (left).* Though cat-like, the genet is related to civets and mongooses. *Below left:* the common duiker *(Sylvicapra grimmia),* again a mainly nocturnal animal. *Below:* the wary and cunning black-backed jackal *(Canus mesomelas). Bottom:* a trio of blesbok *(Damaliscus dorcas phillipsi),* with their distinctive white markings on head, rump and legs. These antelope are grazers, and keep to the more open, grassland country.

135

Above right: the Sybrand van Niekerk resort at Swadini, near Blydepoort, is one of two popular holiday centres in the Blyde River Canyon Nature Reserve. Its caravanning and camping sites are supplemented by a number of well-equipped family chalets. *Right:* Swadini's giant sandstone cliffs. The Blyde River Canyon itself is the centrepiece of the reserve – one of Africa's loveliest. Visitors can drive along the gorge's western edge to take in stunning views of the 'chasm measureless to man' and beyond, through great gaps in the formations, to the plains of the Lowveld.

Not all the Escarpment's attractions, however, are on the grand scale: the area is home to a fascinating variety of plants, birds, insects and small animals. *Above:* A colourful and colour-changing chameleon. *Opposite page, clockwise from top left: Adenium obesum,* the impala lily or 'Sabie Star'; a pair of mating *Acraea natalica* butterflies; the butterflies *Nepheronia argia varia (left)* and *Spindasis natalensis;* a scarlet-chested sunbird feeding on *Schotia brachypetala,* and a white-bellied sunbird savouring *Aloe chibaudii.*

136

Wildlife miscellany. *Anti-clockwise from opposite page, top left:* the famed martial eagle; the ancient, ungainly and fascinating *Adansonia digitata*, or baobab tree; *Ardea melanocephala*, the black-headed heron; the agile klipspringer in its rocky habitat; a pair of warthogs; a pair of blue cranes, usually seen in twosomes, occasionally in flocks (some South Africans keep these birds as garden pets, but generally it is unwise to do so, especially if there are young children in the family: blue cranes have sharp beaks, can be aggressive, and tend to go for the eyes); and below, a lively little vervet monkey.
Overleaf: Lowveld sunrise at Londolozi Game Reserve.

Index

Page numbers in bold refer to illustrations.

The mists, mysteries and magnificence of God's Window. From this high cleft in the Escarpment there are breathtaking views of the Lowveld plains.